Start at the Bone:

Healing For Our Churches and Ourselves

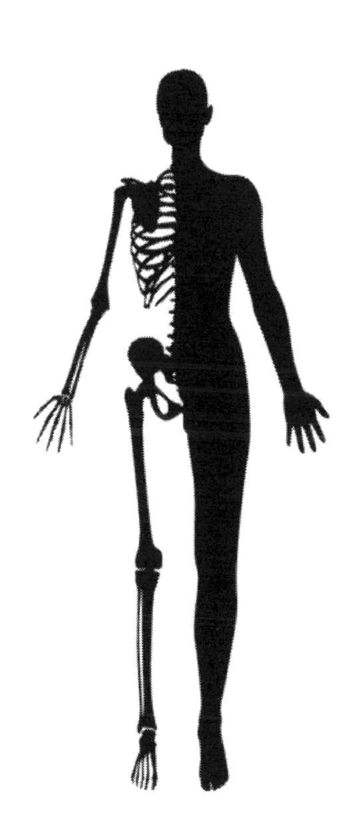

Melissa Fields

2020

TABLE OF CONTENTS

Acknowledgments

My deepest appreciation to my mother, Sarah Fields, for believing in me and reading these chapters as I wrote them. You served as my set of second eyes and an editor, and for that, I am blessed and grateful.

To my father, Steven W. Fields, the President of Stable Ministries and Evangelistic Association, INC., for your leadership and ministry.

To my children, Andrew and Tim Crawford, for encouraging me to pursue my dreams! I am so proud of both of you for using your talents and gifts in God's kingdom.

To my church family at Manville Holiness Church in Gate City, Virginia, for praying with me and for me, for being pillars of your community, and for your devotion to God and His work. To Pastor Deon Turner, my sincerest gratitude for your leadership and willingness to take me under your wing in ministry.

To my amazing friend, Kathi Shaffer, who read the introduction for me and encouraged me to complete this project.

To Michael Wilson and Andrew Crawford for providing feedback and perspective on the sensitive subject matter found in Chapter 10.

To my lifelong teacher and friend, Carol McMurray, for graciously proofreading the first printed copy of this book and for being a source of inspiration to me since my sophomore year in high school.

To Bekah Haren and Beth Cohen, my friends and colleagues, who provided feedback in the last stages of the writing process.

I thank the kind people at Public Domain Vectors (https://publicdomainvectors.org) for the illustrations throughout this book, and Amazon for making this project a reality.

To Shutterstock for the perfect image for the cover!

Most important, I thank my Lord and Savior, Who was, and is, and is to come. Amen.

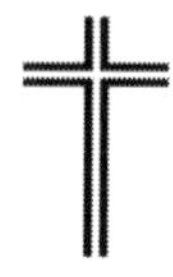

Preface: A Story of Bones

In June of 2019, startling noises coming from the woods prompted three siblings to implore their dad to investigate. At first, their father thought that what they were hearing was the cry of a wounded animal. What happened upon their exploration was heart wrenching. They realized they were hearing a baby's cry and called 9-1-1. The video footage of the tender paramedic delivering the tiny newborn from her plastic bag cocoon took the world by storm. As she cried, he gently soothed her saying, "I'm so sorry. You're a sweetheart. I'm so sorry."

A painful story of rejection. Can you imagine being discarded in such a way? I do not ask that as a judgment against her mother. I have no idea what sort of situation that woman was in, but what I do know is that little girl came into this world and was promptly abandoned by people who were supposed to care for her. What could she do? She was so small. She was helpless, rejected, and left for dead in the woods of Georgia. Thankfully, God, in His miraculous wisdom, has designed humans with an extraordinary capacity to survive. The medical world explains that nature "has given newborn babies the ability to survive for a period of time with no care whatsoever. If abandoned, their body will simply go into a state similar to hibernation--breathing, heart rate, and body functions slow way down--and they can survive this way for about seven or eight days." Tragically, after those few days, "their natural resources will run out," and "Death quickly follows" (Massengale 249).

Isn't it amazing that God has built in a system to protect and sustain us when the world tries to kill us? We are not rejected; we are protected. Baby India, as the child quickly came to be called, was spared an agonizing death. What is even more remarkable is that this tiny newborn who was helpless, small, abandoned, and seemingly forgotten started a chain reaction. People came from everywhere inquiring about how they could adopt her. Hearts were opened to love, and the conversation of adoption began. Some adoption advocates pointed out that while not all of the thousands of people who were willing to adopt Baby India could take her home, they could become parents to many other children who needed loving homes. Due to this infant's abandonment, many children were given the hope of a family and a new life with parents who loved them. Never discount what we can do in our smallness, in our helplessness, in our seeming insignificance. Baby India changed the lives of everyone who knew her, and she changed the face of the foster world.

One reason she was able to survive in that horrific plastic bag is the fact that she, like all babies, was born with 300 malleable bones. As we age, our bones change and we go through the processes of ossification and resorption; as we grow into adults, our bones fuse together so that we only have 206 bones. The malleable bones allow the baby to come through the birth canal smoothly and to curl into a fetal position. Baby India was able to curl up in that bag which in turn helped her to "better regulate [her] body temperature" thereby using "less energy trying to maintain warmth" (Boba). Yes, God designed Baby India to withstand a calamitous beginning until help arrived.

Her story reminds me of another rejected baby whose parents could not even find a suitable place to bring Him into this world. Mary delivered her baby and laid Him in a manger, a feeding trough for animals, because no one would or could give the young couple a room for the night. As she held His tiny body and lovingly wrapped Him in swaddling clothes, I am sure Mary thought about the future her miracle baby would bring. He was so tiny. He was so small. Yet she knew, for the angel Gabriel had told her, "He will save His people." Mary might not have known everything that would take place over the next 33 years, but she did know two things for sure. His name was Jesus, and He would save His people.

If you do not know anything about Him, start with that truth. Start with His name. Our God has a name. It is Jesus. Baby India was given a code name, a nickname. The world knew her by this pseudonym, but Jesus has always been Emmanuel: God with us. Like Baby India's birth, His frantic delivery in a stable would change the foster world, too. He would save all of us and give us new parentage, for no one comes to the Father except through Him (John 14:6). A tiny, rejected human. So small. Who would have ever imagined the impact? His story is a story of salvation, a story of love, a story of protection, and interestingly enough...a story of bones.

He was born with 300 bones, just like us, and because those bones were malleable, Mary could swaddle Him and lay him in the manger. The wise men found Him when He was two, and His bones were still developing. He had not yet stepped into His calling, but the wise men recognized Him as royal. The men in Jerusalem met Him at the age of 12, when His bones were fully developed and fused together. At that time, He stood up and taught in the temple. His parents scolded Him when they had to return to the city to find Him, but He had stepped into His calling at that time and asked, "Know ye not that I must be about my Father's business?" His ministry launched when He was 30 years old, and three and a half years later, our Emmanuel carried His cross up Golgotha's hill. He endured the cross, and not one single bone was broken, for He lovingly laid down His life; the Roman centurions did not have to break His legs in order to expedite His death. He had already freely given His life for ours.

At that time in Jerusalem, bodies were laid in a family tomb, and when only a skeleton remained, the bones were placed in an ossuary. Ossuaries are often used where burial space is scarce. A body is first buried in a temporary grave and after several years, the skeletal remains are placed in the ossuary, or bone box. And here, His story takes the most beautiful plot twist of all time. He never needed more than that temporary grave. Look for His ossuary and you will not find it. No one could break His bones while He was on the cross; no one could place them in a box after decomposition, for He is alive and well!

His story, and ours, is a story of bones. If we want to grow as Christians, and if we want to see our churches heal, we must start at the bone.

REFLECTION:

Throughout this book, I have provided places for you to stop and reflect. Some questions are very personal in nature and you may or may not wish to share your responses in a group setting. You will also find plenty of scriptures to study as you trace the analogy of bones with me. I encourage you to take notes in your book, and you will find ample space to do so. Enjoy your journey!

1. What types of healing do you need to experience: Emotional? Spiritual? Financial? Other types?

2. In what ways does your church need healing? How can you help?

3. In what ways would you like to grow?

4. If you had to describe the story of your life, how would you describe it?

5. In literature, the ending of the story is often called the resolution. What do you want your story's resolution to be?

Introduction

Proverbs 29:18 is one of the most often quoted scriptures, declaring, "Where there is no vision, the people perish!" As eloquent and provocative as those eight words are, I cannot help but think that so many of us are walking around wounded because we have all sorts of vision problems. Distorted vision, tunnel vision, impaired vision, farsighted vision. Surely, this distortion is not what the Lord had in mind when He breathed this proverb into His called writer. Furthermore, according to Jesus, we are not supposed to perish; we are supposed to live an abundant life. Yet the walking wounded, those battle-scarred spiritual warriors, continue to limp into churches and places of worship week in and week out and still can't catch that abundant vision.

How did this happen? Why can't we glimpse God's glorious plan? Could it be that we simply don't view His creation properly? Do we even see ourselves as He sees us? Could it be that we are so dry, so worn-out, so terribly tired because we do not understand the power we can access? Could it be, perhaps, that the whole church is suffering from an identity crisis because its members do not even see and certainly do not know who they are?

In my work as a minister for Stable Ministries and Evangelistic Association, founded by my father, Steven W. Fields, one task I'm commissioned to help carry out is the stabilizing of churches that have withstood hardships, endured trauma, and moved toward recovery. One principle that I have discovered in this work is that many members of churches in recovery must redefine themselves. They must begin to see themselves as the wonderful handiwork of God. By properly aligning their notions of themselves with God's vision of them, individuals can redefine themselves in a healthy way, perpetuating healing in the church from the inside out. According to Jesus, after all, rivers of living water must flow from out of our bellies. If healing is going to come, if flowing waters are going to gush, it has to start at the Church's core. It has to start at the bone.

If you read my first book, *The Trouble with Sticks*, you know that holidays have been a double-edged sword for me. However, as we embark upon the Christmas season, I am excited to begin penning the words that the Lord distinctly told me to write. I begin this book having just served as a minister in a revival for a church I hold dear: Manville Holiness Church, pastored by a former evangelist to Ireland and a profound preacher of the Gospel, Pastor Deon Turner.

I am going to begin by sharing the message of healing and restoration that I delivered behind Manville's sacred desk, and I hope that you can apply the words of healing to your own life so that you can begin to fulfill the commission that God has placed in your heart. All of us are called to the Great Commission (testifying to others the wonderful works of God), so even if you do not know exactly what you are supposed to do for Him, you can begin there.

Join me in Virginia as I deliver the namesake message of this book: “Start at the Bone!”

Manville Holiness Church in Gate City, Virginia

Chapter One

Start at the Bone

Don't be impressed with your own wisdom. Instead, fear the LORD and turn away from evil. Then you will have healing for your body and strength for your bones-Proverbs 3:7-8 (NLT)

In John 4:24 Jesus tells the woman of Samaria, "God is a **Spirit** and they that worship him must worship him in spirit and truth." In Luke 24:39, the resurrected Christ says to Thomas "See my hands and my feet, that it is I myself; touch Me and see for a **spirit** does not have flesh and bones as you see that I have." Friend, if we are to be renewed, we have to deny the flesh and bones by substituting Spirit and Truth in their place. That is what it is going to take to make our churches, our communities, and us whole.

I would like to take my text from Acts 3:1-7 (KJV):

1 Now Peter and John went up together into the temple at the hour of prayer, being the ninth hour.

2 And a certain man lame from his mother's womb was carried, whom they laid daily at the gate of the temple which is called Beautiful, to ask alms of them that entered into the temple;

3 Who seeing Peter and John about to go into the temple asked an alms.

4 And Peter, fastening his eyes upon him with John, said, Look on us.

5 And he gave heed unto them, expecting to receive something of them.

6 Then Peter said, Silver and gold have I none; but such as I have give I thee: In the name of Jesus Christ of Nazareth rise up and walk.

7 And he took him by the right hand, and lifted him up: and immediately his feet and ankle bones received strength.

I really want to draw your attention to verse 7; the writer records that immediately the beggar's feet and ankle bones received strength. I have a message of revival for you-a message of renewal. With the Lord's help, I would like to teach on this thought: Start at the bone!

It is important to note that Jesus Himself explained to Thomas that our flesh and bones distinguish us from God (who is a Spirit). I find it no surprise then that when Peter and John came upon the lame man, the part that needed strengthening was the part of him that was not like God. God in His infinite wisdom understands that when He holds the parts of us that are not like Him, He can impart His strength and His virtue to us so that real change can come. When Peter and John's words came forth, the Holy Ghost in them knew exactly where to start. He started at the bone. The part of Peter and John that was God's essence, His Spirit, His Holy Ghost, encountered the part of the man that was not like God. My friend, revival happens like that! If revival is to come, it will not come through a man or a woman who is not filled with His Holy Spirit because, you see, we are just flesh and bone. We are not like God. We are made in His image, but until His Spirit takes over our flesh, saturates our bones, and directs our minds, then we can do nothing. Peter and John did not have this kind of power when they were traveling with Jesus because they had Him with them. Their group grew from 12 to 72, and they did have some power, but the revival started when the Jesus movement climbed from 120 to over 3,000 in the span of a few hours. When Peter walked with God INSIDE of him instead of walking with God BESIDE of him, the parts of Peter that were not like God gave way to the Holy Ghost. The Spirit gave Peter the boldness and the power to do things that He had never done before and to go places where he might not be welcomed.

As a matter of fact, in those days, the Gate called Beautiful was a strategic place for a beggar to be because it was customary for people to place their offerings in the treasury as they passed through the gate, but notice what Peter said: "Silver and gold have I none." What? He dared to enter the gate called Beautiful without an offering, without so much as a coin? Yes, he did. Why? Because he had the baptism of the Holy Ghost. Friends, the Holy Spirit will take you through gates, across rivers, and through valleys that you never thought you could go through. How? By starting at the bone-the human parts of you that are not like God-and this process fully transforms you. Regeneration will embolden you.

Talk about a man who needed revival-who needed renewal! Peter was such a one! Just a few weeks prior to the story of his encounter with this lame man, Peter was denying his Lord. He saw the disciples scattered and hiding, women weeping, and Jesus crucified. He knew he was a sinful man. He had lost all hope. What then turned him into a man who could boldly walk through the beautiful gate without so much as a silver drachma and declare to the lame feeble man, "Rise up and walk in the name of Jesus"? Revival! What revived him? The Holy Ghost! His upper room experience! Consider what happened on the Day of Pentecost, 50 days after Christ's resurrection:

Acts 2: And when the day of Pentecost was fully come, they were all with one accord in one place.

2 And suddenly there came a sound from heaven as of a rushing mighty wind, and it filled all the house where they were sitting.

3 And there appeared unto them cloven tongues like as of fire, and it sat upon each of them.

4 And they were all filled with the Holy Ghost, and began to speak with other tongues, as the Spirit gave them utterance. (KJV)

The Holy Spirit regenerated Peter. Did regeneration make him perfect? No. Nevertheless, it did transform him from a man who denied his relationship with Christ into a man who proclaimed "Rise up and walk!" That same Holy Spirit that was poured out on the Day of Pentecost touched the lame man's bones and strengthened him. God, operating through Peter, started at the bone.

From the very beginning, in fact, God started at the bone. When God created man from the dust of the ground, He breathed life into Adam. Adam's name in the Hebrew means "human." God had created something **new**. Humankind was born. However, when God saw that it was not good for the man to be alone, He decided to take what He had made new and **renew** it. How did He do that? He reached in, took "bone of Adam's bone," and made humanity new again by creating the female. Why did God renew humanity with the bone? Why start with the bone?

To answer the questions, we must research bones just a bit. You see, bones are more than just the scaffolding that holds the body together. Bones come in all shapes and sizes and have many roles. Bones, in fact, are analogous to the Church. Paul teaches that all members are unique and have their own function within the body. He even likens the Church to body parts in 1 Corinthians 12. Yes, bones are truly unique. In fact, despite first impressions, bones are living, active tissues that are constantly changing. To remain healthy and strong, they must constantly engage in "remodeling" (Newman). This concept is certainly true of the Church as well.

Considering that truth, we can answer the question concerning why God reached into Adam and pulled out bone to create the woman. Quite simply, the bone is living, active, and constantly remodeling. He pulled new beauty from the original and created Eve, whose name translates to "life." Doesn't that make perfect sense? When we put Adam and Eve's names together, we get "human life." All because God breathed into Adam and made him a living, active person! It comes as no surprise, then, that Adam was so busy in the garden, God had to put him into a deep sleep in order to renew humankind.

When is the last time that God put you to sleep, so to speak? Sometimes when people or churches have some healing or strengthening to do, they will fall into a period of inactivity. This inactivity is often frustrating to us because we are conditioned to be a busy, productive society. Sometimes, this conditioning even causes people to judge churches or members. They might murmur, "That church isn't really doing anything," or "That brother or sister really needs to get busy!" However, sometimes God has to force us to rest, be still, sleep deeply, and let Him create. Adam certainly was not busy or doing anything when God renewed all of humanity. He was asleep while God was operating.

When we go silent, when we go into a deep sleep, God operates. Sometimes, in order to revive, we have to experience a period of rest and recovery. How many of you have ever been hurt so deeply, that you just had to back away from the hustle and bustle of life for a while? How many of you have ever been wounded in church, and you just needed to sleep for a bit? Sleep has healing powers. God might let a church sleep for a bit, but what about the bones of the congregation, those faithful people who hold up her framework and never leave? God's renewal starts with them.

Don't be discouraged by periods of inactivity in your life. Those times might be an indication that God is operating behind the scenes just as He did that day in the Garden of Eden. Of course, God's operation was successful. The bone that He pulled out of Adam had many functions. Bones hold the body together, they protect vital organs, and they allow us to move. Thus, it makes sense that God, in renewing His churches, would start with the bones.

Several years ago, my father wrote a powerful song about the valley of dry bones in the Old Testament. In Ezekiel's vision of that valley, those dry bones, sleeping and inanimate, represented Israel. Let's take a look at the text from Ezekiel 37:1-10:

1 The hand of the LORD was upon me, and carried me out in the spirit of the LORD, and set me down in the midst of the valley which was full of bones,

2 And caused me to pass by them round about: and, behold, there were very many in the open valley; and, lo, they were very dry.

3 And he said unto me, Son of man, can these bones live? And I answered, O Lord GOD, thou knowest.

4 Again he said unto me, Prophesy upon these bones, and say unto them, O ye dry bones, hear the word of the LORD.

5 Thus saith the Lord GOD unto these bones; Behold, I will cause breath to enter into you, and ye shall live:

6 And I will lay sinews upon you, and will bring up flesh upon you, and cover you with skin, and put breath in you, and ye shall live; and ye shall know that I am the LORD.

7 So I prophesied as I was commanded: and as I prophesied, there was a noise, and behold a

shaking, and the bones came together, bone to his bone.

8 And when I beheld, lo, the sinews and the flesh came up upon them, and the skin covered them above: but there was no breath in them.

9 Then said he unto me, Prophesy unto the wind, prophesy, son of man, and say to the wind, Thus saith the Lord GOD; Come from the four winds, O breath, and breathe upon these slain, that they may live.

10 So I prophesied as he commanded me, and the breath came into them, and they lived, and stood up upon their feet, an exceeding great army. (KJV)

God doesn't raise up armies to be inactive. Instead, God begins with His people, and then His people affect everyone who encounters them! You might be at rest in a valley now, but I assure you that when the wind of God blows on you again, He will lift you up to activity!

Let's go back to our original text in Acts. I want you to see Peter and John as the bones of the church. Like bones, they are lively, they are active, and they are supportive. They are helping one another to hold up the new movement, protecting the vital organ of the truth of Christ's resurrection: moving, moving, moving! They are always on the move. Always preaching Christ. Furthermore, they are renewed. The wind of the Holy Spirit has already breathed on them. However, the man outside of the temple has given up. He is on the ground, unable to move. He represents those on the outside of the temple that have slumped over, stuck and unable to rise. God is telling us to start at the bone. To be renewed and to help those who have not stepped into spirit and truth, who are still bound by flesh and bone. He is rousing us from our sleep. He is commanding our dry bones to live again so that we can help the ones who are stuck outside of the gate!

I delivered that message in a revival to a specific congregation at a specific time, but when you think about it, the truth applies to all of us who call ourselves part of God's Church. If the body is going to work as a whole, if it is going to be able to sustain life, it must have a strong infrastructure. You and I comprise that structure. In order to help the lost, we must find ourselves.

REFLECTION:

1. Considering the analogy from Ezekiel, would you characterize yourself as having dry bones or lively bones? Explain.

2. How has God previously moved for you or your church during times of inactivity?

3. Are you currently experiencing inactivity? How can you use this time to draw closer to God?

Chapter Two

Overcome Your Identity Crisis

"Before I formed you in the womb I knew you, before you were born I set you apart...-Jeremiah 1:5 (NIV)

I will never forget my grandmother or the day that we said our final good-bye. Gran was 88 years-old and was the jolliest person I ever was blessed to know. For years, our relationship grew stronger and stronger as every Friday was "Granny night." On Fridays, I would take her supper to her and we would eat together. Then she and I would spend the evening talking, playing games, watching television, or just sitting together. Inevitably, one or both of us would get so comfortable in each other's company and her cozy den that we would just drift off to sleep.

Some weeks, other family members joined us. Her great-grandchildren would sometimes come and nothing pleased her more. We would play rounds and rounds of Bingo or Sorry and just enjoy each other. Often, my oldest brother Brian would visit as well. He would bring movies that she loved to watch. At the end of the workweek, I was tired, and every now and then, I silently grumbled about going. I'm ashamed of that now. However, I am glad to say that I always made the effort to go no matter how I felt because I didn't know how long I would have this precious soul in my life. My children were especially blessed to have their great-grandmother with them as they launched into adulthood. Nevertheless, as the years crept by, I knew eventually I would have to say good-bye to one of the greatest friends I ever had.

In December of 2018, she became very ill and was admitted to a nursing facility after spending some time in the hospital. We were hopeful that physical therapy would allow her to come home to us. She never did. On August 8 of the following year, the Lord called her home on my cousin Misty's birthday. All of us were devastated even though we knew that this day was looming. We buried Granny on a beautiful, sunny Sunday morning. The date was August 11 of 2019 when I said my final good-bye. I sat beside my dad and just wept as Reverend Christopher G. Fields, my brother, spoke a final word over her graveside.

As God ordained, I was scheduled to speak that evening at a local church, Victory Tabernacle Pentecostal Church, and I did not want to cancel even though my heart was heavy. Gran always supported my ministry, and I knew that she would not want me to cancel a speaking engagement. So... I put one foot in front of the other, wiped away the tears, and went to tell that congregation what I'm about to tell you.

I was scheduled to speak for the next three nights, and God dealt with me to talk to His Church-His Bride-about her identity crisis. At the time, I did not know that 2020 was also going to ask America to take a hard look at herself and decide who She is. Her answer will depend upon how We the People decide whose image we are created in.

Maybe you need to redefine yourself. Maybe you have your own identity crisis to conquer. If so, I invite you to join me at Victory Tabernacle Pentecostal Church, pastored by Donald Madden, as I deliver the first message in the three part series: *Identity Crisis*

Victory Tabernacle Pentecostal Church
Kingsport, Tennessee

Part One: Who They Say I am

Church, I am honored to bring the word of the Lord to you today. Your pastor called me when my grandmother passed away, and he wanted to know if I still planned to come. He reached out very kindly to me, but I assured him that I did not want to miss the opportunity to address this congregation. My grandmother held the Word of God as sacred. She read it every day until she went to the nursing home. She would want me to speak to you this evening. In fact, she would insist, because the message is urgent. I am convinced that if the church of the living God is ever going to become the force in this world that it is destined to become, its members are going to have to realize who they are in Christ. With that thought in mind, I would like to deliver a series of messages to you that deals specifically with the identity crisis that the Church of the Living God has found itself in. I want to speak to you about who the world says you are, who God says you are, and who you say you are. To begin, let's go to the Book of Judges, chapter 11: 1-8.

11 Now Jephthah the Gileadite was a mighty man of valour, and he was the son of an harlot: and Gilead begat Jephthah.

2 And Gilead's wife bare him sons; and his wife's sons grew up, and they thrust out Jephthah, and

said unto him, Thou shalt not inherit in our father's house; for thou art the son of a strange woman.

3 Then Jephthah fled from his brethren, and dwelt in the land of Tob: and there were gathered vain men to Jephthah, and went out with him.

4 And it came to pass in process of time, that the children of Ammon made war against Israel.

5 And it was so, that when the children of Ammon made war against Israel, the elders of Gilead went to fetch Jephthah out of the land of Tob:

6 And they said unto Jephthah, Come, and be our captain, that we may fight with the children of Ammon.

7 And Jephthah said unto the elders of Gilead, Did not ye hate me, and expel me out of my father's house? and why are ye come unto me now when ye are in distress?

8 And the elders of Gilead said unto Jephthah, Therefore we turn again to thee now, that thou mayest go with us, and fight against the children of Ammon, and be our head over all the inhabitants of Gilead.

I want you to notice something in particular about Jephthah. The Bible says that he was a mighty man of valor **AND** a son of a prostitute. His family cast him out. They rejected him! They wanted nothing to do with him, and instead of telling himself that he was a mighty man of valor, he identified with what they said about him in verse 2: "Thou art the son of a strange woman." Talk about discrimination! Talk about unfairness! Jephthah could not control his parentage. He had no say in his father's decision to be unfaithful, nor did he choose his mother's vocation. What he could respond to, however, was what God said about him-that he was a mighty man of valor. Being honorable. Being valiant. Being mighty. Those are choices. He was not weak. There was nothing wrong with him; his family was just choosing which part of him they would focus on. Sadly, instead of standing up to them, Jephthah gave in to the idea of who they said he was. This type of behavior is dangerous because it inevitably creates an identity crisis.

We have to know what God says about us. We have to know what parts of us God wants to develop and which parts we need to overcome and discard. When we start listening to what they say about us, whoever "they" might be, we actually become what they say. Consider this: the Bible says Jephthah fled from his home and family. He ran. Does that sound like a mighty man of valor to you? They robbed him of his true identity. He was hurt and rejected, and he gave in to what they said about him and began to behave in a way that did not line up with what the Lord had said. Mighty, valiant men do not run. Yet, in this story, Jephthah fled from his brothers (in a total identity crisis) and made his home in the land of Tob.

Now, I want you to see the chain reaction. He fell in with a crowd of "vain fellows" which is our translation's way of saying scoundrels or ruffians. Apparently, he began to surround himself with people who would not be characterized as mighty men of valor at all. He was living on the east of Jordan in the middle of nowhere. Tob is not known as anything special. It isn't a capital city. It lies on the outskirts of Syria. In fact, many biblical scholars today say the site is unknown. Essentially Jephthah's identity crisis has led him to be an outcast in the middle of nowhere! All of his valor, all of his might, was being wasted simply because he chose to believe what they said about him.

Still, one thing I like about Jephthah is this: He was not idle. Ironically, the land of Tob means "good," and God was going to bring something good out of this situation. Yes, he fell in with some scoundrels, but he didn't follow them. Instead, he became their leader. They "went out with him," the Bible says. According to biblical scholars, this ring of men and Jephthah practiced warfare and became a force to be reckoned with. Their reputation, in fact, eventually led his brothers to come crawling back to him. You see, when push comes to shove, people will recognize your talents; they will recognize your anointing: soon enough, despite the fact that you feel invisible, they are going to come looking for you because they need what only you can offer.

The story of Jephthah reminds me of another man who fled and was surrounded by a formidable group of men. How many of you know that David was also despised by his brothers? They called him a troublemaker, and they were jealous of his anointing. His own father didn't even bother to call him back to the house when Samuel came to anoint the next king. No one thought that the least among Jesse's sons would be the young man Samuel was looking for. Even David's father in essence said, "You are just fit to carry bread to your brothers and to keep the flock." However, David knew there was something more to serving God. His brother said, "You are just a troublemaker. Give us our food and leave!" Not David! He stayed to defend God against a blasphemous giant. He chose not to listen to what his brother said about him. He chose not to listen to what his father said about him. He chose to let the warrior rise up in him, and he slew the giant!

Later, when Saul was chasing him, David and his small band of men were living in caves; despite that, the young giant killer knew he was a king. Let me tell you something. Your situation might not look like what you want it to look like right now. You might know that God has called you and your church to do more. If that is the case, my advice to you is to listen to what God is saying about you and your calling instead of what some people in your family or some people outside of the house of God are saying about you. Fill yourself with the Word that tells you who you are, for you are fearfully and wonderfully made, you are created in His own image. Do you not know that God so loved you that He came into this world to offer Himself as a sacrifice for you? You might be living in a cave now, but if God said you are a king, you are a king!

Of course, Jephthah's brothers finally came looking for him. They needed his anointing. Thankfully, during all of that time he had been away from them, he had been honing his skills as a warrior. He traveled to a good place and did not sit down. He worked. He led. He learned. Even though he was leading people that he might not have chosen, and even though he was living in a land away from his rightful home,

God said, “I’ve placed you in Tob, in a good land, and I’ve redefined you. You are what I said you were from the beginning. You are a mighty man of valor, and I am going to raise you up in front of your brothers and everyone else. You will defeat the Ammonites!”

If you know the story of Jephthah, then you know that he made a costly mistake later on. I blame it on his identity crisis yet again. You can go back and read the entirety of chapter 11 and you will see that without question, God was on Jephthah’s side. Furthermore, God had already made him a mighty man of valor. Then in verse 29, as Jephthah prepared to enter into his final battle, the Spirit of the Lord came upon him. I am perplexed by what happens next. Despite the fact that the Spirit of the Lord was upon him, Jephthah decided that he needed to vow a vow in order to secure victory. Consider verses 29-31:

29 Then the Spirit of the Lord came upon Jephthah, and he passed over Gilead, and Manasseh, and passed over Mizpeh of Gilead, and from Mizpeh of Gilead he passed over unto the children of Ammon.

30 And Jephthah vowed a vow unto the Lord, and said, If thou shalt without fail deliver the children of Ammon into mine hands,

31 Then it shall be, that whatsoever cometh forth of the doors of my house to meet me, when I return in peace from the children of Ammon, shall surely be the Lord's, and I will offer it up for a burnt offering. (KJV)

My question is this: Why did he even feel it was necessary to strike a bargain with God? God was obviously on his side. Yet, this is the traumatic end of the story:

34 And Jephthah came to Mizpeh unto his house, and, behold, his daughter came out to meet him with timbrels and with dances: and she was his only child; beside her he had neither son nor daughter.

35 And it came to pass, when he saw her, that he rent his clothes, and said, Alas, my daughter! thou hast brought me very low, and thou art one of them that trouble me: for I have opened my mouth unto the Lord, and I cannot go back. (KJV)

He lost his daughter, and none of these tragic events needed to happen. If he had just believed what God had said. If he had just moved with the Spirit of the Lord. If he had just spoken life and said to himself, "I'm enough. I don't need to vow a vow. The Spirit of God is on me. I'm anointed. I'm ready for this!" Unfortunately, he did not. In his doubting of himself and his God, he said, "If thou shalt without fail deliver." Let's stop and examine those six little words, shall we?

First, the Lord is not going to fail. Therefore, the vow was completely unsanctioned. Friends, if we do not start believing in what God has said about us, if we do not learn to follow the Spirit when it comes upon us, if we do not learn to trust God, we will pay a heavy price. Listen to me very closely. Lean in and listen. You are enough. You don't need to add to God's plan. Go forth in your anointing and don't vow unnecessary vows, don't make unnecessary promises, don't beg God not to fail. He won't!

How do you define yourself? Make sure your definition lines up with that part of you that God wants to develop. Jephthah struggled with his identity because of who his mother was. He struggled with part of himself, and we all do. Paul wrote about daily struggling to crucify the flesh, but struggle produces anointing and strength. After all, Jephthah's isolation, his banishment, his rejection developed the gifts that God had already given him.

True, people might say unflattering things about you. Yes, they might focus on a part of you that isn't the part you want to develop or that God is going to use. Don't listen. Who they say you are is none of your business. If you think you are different from the rest of us, let me submit this truth to you. They even treated our Lord the way Jephthah's people treated him. Go with me to the Book of Mark and let's read the first three verses of chapter 6:

1 And he went out from thence, and came into his own country; and his disciples follow him.

2 And when the sabbath day was come, he began to teach in the synagogue: and many hearing him were astonished, saying, From whence hath this man these things? and what wisdom is this which is given unto him, that even such mighty works are wrought by his hands?

3 Is not this the carpenter, the son of Mary, the brother of James, and Joses, and of Juda, and Simon? and are not his sisters here with us? And they were offended at him. (KJV)

He was the Most High, God in the flesh, and they chose to focus on a part of him that was not even going to be developed. He did not come to be a carpenter; He was the Savior of the world! Thankfully, Jesus did not listen to their negativity. He knew who He was. From at least the age of 12, He knew that He had divine business to take care of.

People could say these things about me: She is a divorced woman with few friends and even fewer possessions. She is a struggling teacher trying to make ends meet. She battles depression and is weak and vulnerable. All of those things might be true, but they are not what God has decided to develop in me. He says, "You are my faithful servant and highly favored. I trust you with My word. You are a speaker of My truth, and I love you." He says, "You are a writer and a teacher. That is the part of you I want to develop."

What parts of you can you give to God? What does He say about you? Do not trust your heart, for emotions will move it. Do not always trust the words of others, for they do not know God's divine plan for your life. Ask Him today to help you redefine yourself so that you can see yourself as He intends!

It might surprise my readers to learn that I do suffer from depression. In fact, I endured it far too long before I sought help, but in all of my suffering, God kept me. When I finally learned that treating depression is a lifestyle, I was liberated from its clutches. God brought me from a suicide attempt as a teenager, from a struggling single mom who couldn't get out of bed some days, to a joy-filled, spirit-filled Minister of His Gospel. How? By putting good friends in my life who directed me to get the help that I needed, and by pouring His Word, His truth, into my soul.

When you can believe the truth that God says about you, you can rise above depression by following the plan that is set before you. If that plan involves medication, counseling, and spiritual guidance, there is nothing wrong with that. Work your plan! God is the Master Planner, after all. However, let me caution you that any plan absent of Him is destined to fail. To know who you are, you have to know the One who made you.

If you are suffering from depression, anxiety, or both, I encourage you first to get into God's Word. Then surround yourself with a support network. That network should probably include your physician, close friends, and family. Ideally, it would also extend to your church family. Every day, determine in your heart to believe that you are loved and worthwhile. You will need to remind yourself of this regularly. You might need to come back to these chapters often and revisit them. To be honest with you, I have to remind myself constantly that God loves me, and that I am not alone. You and I, precious friend, must refuse to stay in an identity crisis. God says that He knew you before He formed you in the womb. You were worth the agony of the cross for Him. Remind yourself who you really are and to whom you truly belong!

REFLECTION:

1. What aspects of your identity do you think God can develop for His kingdom?

2. What aspects of your character need refinement?

3. What are some active steps you can take to bring about positive change?

4. Are you currently struggling with clinical depression? What active steps can you take to manage and/or overcome your depression?

My grandmother, Betty Winegar Carroll, in 2018 (left)
Gran and I on July 4, 2019, before her passing (right)
We shared a love of music, a love for the Lord, and a love for each other.
Surrounding yourself with supportive, loving people is priceless.

Chapter Three

Lift Your Voice!

For the stone will cry out from the wall, and the beam from the woodwork respond-
Habakkuk 2:11 (ESV)

I think one reason that I suffered so long from depression was my low self-esteem and skewed body image. Let's face it. The media constantly bombards both men and women with society's ideal picture of beauty. Even when I was young with a girlish figure, I didn't think I measured up, and if I didn't think I measured up then, you can imagine how I felt in my 30s and 40s after having two children and raising them as a single mom. My negative self-image did little to strengthen my walk with God or relationships with those around me. We all know that it is hard to love others when we can't love ourselves, but no matter how hard I tried, I just couldn't.

As I am writing these words, we have found ourselves in a national crisis. It is Good Friday, and the churches have announced that they will remain closed on Easter because of Covid-19. These times are unprecedented. I have lived nearly half of a century, and I have never before witnessed anything like this. Most of us are trying to obey the stay at home orders issued by our respective governors, and so I have been home for several weeks now. One thing I have learned from living alone during Covid-19 is this: You have to love yourself.

You have a few extra pounds? Love yourself.

You have days when you aren't as productive as you would like? Love yourself.

You have days when you napped a little too long? Love yourself.

You have days when you don't feel beautiful? Love yourself.

God knows that if we become too self-absorbed with productivity and perfection, we are going to end up being way too hard on ourselves. This crisis has taught me not to beat myself up. It has also taught me to enjoy my own company. I'm determined to be happy with the lady in the mirror who needs to lose a few pounds and desperately needs to see her hairstylist! If I can love myself right now, I will be ready to extend love to others when this crisis is over. In the meantime, I just need to get up every day and do the best I can. That is all any of us can do, amen?

If anyone in the Bible had to learn to love his own company, it was Paul. Often imprisoned, he focused on others and his ministry rather than his dungeon. Frankly, I am in awe of the man. Paul had the gift of contentment; he learned to be content in any situation. I am 48 and just now learning that. Better late than never.

Like Paul, the Apostle Peter had to learn to forgive himself and be content in his service to God. In fact, the Lord had to ask him three times to feed his sheep, but he finally got the message. The next sermon that I am going to share with you takes its focus from one of Peter's famous letters.

Join me at Victory Pentecostal Tabernacle for the second message in the series: *Identity Crisis.*

Part Two: Who I Say I am

Yesterday, we discussed what others say about us and how their words can lead us into an identity crisis if we fail to recognize the parts of us that God wants to develop. Paul says we are in constant warfare with the flesh; we all have two sides. Sometimes the thing we would not do is the very thing we do, but we have to strive continually to let God work and develop the side of us that He can use for His glory. We talked about Jephthah who was a mighty man of valor and a son of a prostitute. His brothers cast him out because they ignored the mighty, valiant side of him and chose to concentrate on a side of him that he couldn't even control. He listened at first. We talked about David whose father and brothers did not understand that he had potential to be a king developed by God's own hand. They saw only one side to him–a shepherd boy fit to run errands. Finally, we discussed how Jesus' own ministry was limited in His hometown because those who knew Him focused on the wrong parts of His identity. They said, "Is not this the carpenter's son?" The Bible says that He only healed a few in their town because of their unbelief and confusion about who He really was.

The church today is in an identity crisis because its members fail to see their own potential: We are prayer warriors, praise leaders, teachers, preachers, believers, students of the highest God. But we don't always act like we are, do we? With that said, I would like to deliver the second part of this series to you. Moving on from who they say I am, let's now focus on who I say I am.

I'd like to read one scripture of text from the King James Version to get started:

But ye are a chosen generation, a royal priesthood, an holy nation, a peculiar people; that ye should shew forth the praises of him who hath called you out of darkness into his marvellous light...(1 Peter 2:9).

If you are confused about your calling in God and who you are, this verse is an excellent place to start. I hear people all the time saying, "I don't have a calling. I don't have a purpose with God." Yes, you do. Here is where it starts. All of us are chosen to show forth His praise. You are to be a worshipper foremost because your worship lifts Him up, and He said, "If I be lifted up, I will draw all men unto me" (John 12:32). To worship Him, though, you have to learn to open your mouth. To do that, you have to understand who you are. Let me talk to you about some people who had a difficult time opening their mouths. Why? Because they were experiencing a multifaceted identity crisis. They did not understand who God was, and they certainly did not understand who they were.

I would like to look closely at Moses. When God called Moses to go to Egypt and become the deliverer of His people, Moses immediately went into identity crisis mode. First of all, he acted as though he didn't even know who God was even though he spent many years with his natural birth mother (a worshipper of the One True God) before he ever went to live in the palace as Pharaoh's own. He questioned God saying, "But the people. They will want to know who You are. They will want to know your name," as if his Hebrew family had not told him about Yahweh. God simply told him, "I am that I am." He knew Moses understood who was talking to him! Then Moses focused on his shortcomings. He offered all sorts of reasons why he was not what God called him to be. He reasoned, "I cannot speak! I am not eloquent in speech. There is no way, Lord, that I can do what You are asking me to do." So God told him that He would send Aaron with him.

How many of you know that Moses could speak? He was well able to do what God destined him to do. He was who God said he was. He just wasn't ready to admit it. How do I know that? A careful reading of Moses and Aaron's encounters with Pharaoh shows that God eased Moses into his calling by giving him the support of Aaron, who had actually been raised as a slave instead of the son of royalty. In this regard, Aaron became a conduit that served two purposes. First, he was able to endear Moses to his Hebrew relatives, and second, he bolstered Moses' confidence (Farbiarz). Aaron did indeed do most of the talking until after the third plague ceased. However, when the fourth plague descends, we witness Moses finally step into his leadership role, beginning in Exodus 8:26. Up until that point, the account lists Aaron as the one doing most of the direct talking to Pharaoh. After Exodus 8:26, however, we read repeatedly "Moses said." It took Moses some time to figure it out, but he could indeed speak for his God. He could be a mouthpiece for Yahweh. He could offer the praises of the Lord, but he had to redefine who he was. He had to admit, "Yes, I am the deliverer. I am going to have to open my mouth and speak!"

We never learn for sure what sort of impediment that Moses had. Perhaps he stuttered a bit. Perhaps he had a lisp. In fact, "the omniscient biblical narrator provides the descriptions of its other central characters, [but] it is silent on Moses' 'heavy-mouthed and heavy-tongued' condition" mentioned in Exodus 4:10. This silence "implies that Moses' impediment loomed larger in his own mind than as a handicap perceptible to others" (Farbiarz). If you, like Moses, have convinced yourself that you are not capable of doing what God has asked you to do, may I suggest that your mind might be playing tricks on you? All of your supposed shortcomings might be imperceptible to the rest of us. Perhaps you need to surround yourself with people like Aaron, who can help you make the transition into your ordained role.

Now, I would like to look at Jeremiah. The Jewish people know Jeremiah as the second major prophet. He wrote the Book of Jeremiah, the Book of Lamentations, and mostly likely the Book of Kings. God was developing a prophet, a writer, and a worshipper, but let's look at how the prophet first identified himself.

4 Then the word of the Lord came unto me, saying,

5 Before I formed thee in the belly I knew thee; and before thou camest forth out of the womb I sanctified thee, and I ordained thee a prophet unto the nations.

6 Then said I, Ah, Lord God! behold, I cannot speak: for I am a child.

7 But the Lord said unto me, Say not, I am a child: for thou shalt go to all that I shall send thee, and whatsoever I command thee thou shalt speak. (KJV)

Again, we have encountered someone who claims that he is not what God needs, and that he cannot speak, but remember that Paul taught that we are all called to show forth the praises of our God. Do you ever wonder why the signs of the Holy Ghost relate to the tongue? You remember Acts chapter 2? They were speaking in tongues. They were prophesying. They were praying. Why do you suppose the Lord chose the tongue by which to manifest His glory? I think one reason is so that we can never use the excuse that we cannot speak or show forth His praise once He fills us with His Holy Spirit. The most disobedient part of the body, in fact, is the tongue (James 3). It makes perfect sense, then, that when God fills us with His spirit, He declares, "I've got to take hold of your tongue! You have to give Me control of your mouth because too many of My servants have said, 'We cannot speak.'" Oh yes, my friend, He is going to make sure that you speak! He is going to make sure that you open your mouth and use your tongue to show forth His praise.

Long before the events of Acts 2, we read of Jeremiah in an identity crisis. "I'm just a child," he says, but God tells him that is not true. He declares that Jeremiah will step into the role of prophet. We cannot choose the parts of us that we think disqualify us to do what God wants us to do. No, my friends, we must be willing to define ourselves the way God defines us. Not only was Jeremiah a speaker, but he was a visionary. When we read verses 11 and 12, we find his gift at work:

11 Moreover the word of the Lord came unto me, saying, Jeremiah, what seest thou? And I said, I see a rod of an almond tree.

12 Then said the Lord unto me, Thou hast well seen: for I will hasten my word to perform it. (KJV)

Notice that the Lord Himself encourages Jeremiah. "Good job," He says. "You have seen well."

Do you know that the Lord will encourage you? Do you know that right now the Lord can commune with your spirit? When you answer Him and let Him define you, you can respond like my next subject, a servant of God whom many overlook. He was a shepherd who did not focus on the aspects of his life that seemed to suggest he could not fulfill his calling. He simply believed God. God called Amos to prophesy to the Israelites, but they did not always like what he had to say. In fact, Amaziah tried to hush him as we read in chapter 7 of the Book of Amos:

12 Also Amaziah said unto Amos, O thou seer, go, flee thee away into the land of Judah, and there eat bread, and prophesy there:

13 But prophesy not again any more at Bethel: for it is the king's chapel, and it is the king's court.

14 Then answered Amos, and said to Amaziah, I was no prophet, neither was I a prophet's son; but I was an herdman, and a gatherer of sycomore fruit:

15 And the Lord took me as I followed the flock, and the Lord said unto me, Go, prophesy unto my people Israel.

16 Now therefore hear thou the word of the Lord...(KJV).

You can go back to the beginning of the Book of Amos, and you will find no trace of a man caught in an identity crisis. God calls him in chapter 1, and Amos immediately begins to prophesy to his people. He never offers an excuse as to why he could not do what God called him to do. He tells Amaziah, "Look! I was no prophet! I wasn't even born to a prophet. I was a herdsman and a gatherer of fruit, but the Lord took me and made me a prophet. Truly, you need to hear what God is saying!"

Amos opened his mouth, spoke the words of God, and never confused his vocation with his purpose. His purpose in life was to obey God, to worship God, and to speak God's Word. We have the same call to obedience and worship. We can offer excuses like Moses and Jeremiah, or we can simply obey like Amos. I think the choice is clear.

Chapter Four

Be Available

But Jesus said, Suffer little children, and forbid them not, to come unto me: for of such is the kingdom of heaven-Matthew 19:14 (KJV)

In the closing of the last chapter, I mentioned how important obedience is in our walk with God. Truly, our walk with God cannot even begin until we obediently enter into a covenant with Him, eager to carry out our end of the partnership. Just imagine! We have the invitation to become partners with God. In fact, one of the greatest blessings of my spiritual walk has been the opportunity to teach my own Godchildren how to become His partners.

Watching a young person come to Christ is both beautiful and fulfilling. Our young people have an enthusiasm–a spiritual spark–that we adults would do well to emulate. Is it any wonder that the children rushing to Jesus despite the scolding of nearby adults filled Him with joy as He exclaimed, "Suffer the little children to come to me"? They have an earnestness about them and a pure zeal to please their Savior that I have been fortunate to witness firsthand. Recently, in fact, I saw such zeal igniting in a Sunday school classroom and spilling out to the creek behind the church in Manville. In fact, I had the honor of performing my first baptismal service in February of 2020 when two of my Godchildren decided to take on the name of Jesus in water baptism.

I will never forget how the lesson that led to their decisions unfolded. I had asked my class what they wanted to study, and since I have students comprising a broad range in ages, I received quite different answers. My three Godchildren who are in the class gave me three specific requests. Myranda wanted to study Jeremiah 29:11. Gracie wanted to study about Jesus' love for us, and Casey Tanner wanted to study about Noah. I sat down to prepare for Sunday's lesson and wrote each of those items down. "Now...how do I connect the dots?" I thought. Suddenly it occurred to me that one word connected the scriptures each child wanted to study. One word. Covenant!

After all, God made a covenant with Noah never to destroy the Earth again by water. In Jeremiah 29:11, God reminded the people of the covenant He had established with them so that they could have an abundant future. Finally, Jesus brought humanity into covenant with Him as recorded in John 3:16. I immediately prepared for our study. My lesson plan included a description of covenant as a partnership, and we talked about how all of us enter into covenant or partnership with God. I asked the students to jot down on post-it notes what they thought it would look like to be in covenant with the Lord.

They immediately went to work! I have never seen kids write on post-it notes so quickly! As I read their post-its aloud, I noticed that Myranda had written "Be Baptized." I was not sure if Randa had been baptized before I met her, so I asked her about it. She said that she had not. I then asked her if she wanted to be. Let me drive home this point. When I asked her to consider whether she wanted to be baptized, there was no hesitation. There was no resistance. There was no blinking of an eye. This young, beautiful girl said, "YES!" You see, she wanted to be obedient to the word of God that we had studied. She also wanted to claim Jeremiah 29:11 and all of those other beautiful verses that speak of covenant with God. She wanted to be in partnership with Him. What's more, her little brother did as well. Because he is quite a bit younger than Myranda, I wanted to make sure that he understood what it meant. He said, "Yes! It means I love Jesus and want to be His partner." Not long after that class, I took them to the beautiful creek behind the church and baptized them in the lovely name of Jesus as their immediate family and their church family looked on.

When I think of their enthusiasm, their eagerness, their willingness to come to Jesus, I am moved to tears. Children have a way of trusting God and just doing what He asks. Few things in my life have even come close to rivaling the joy I felt when I baptized my God kids. It was as if God said, "Will you come?" They heartily responded, "Yes! Here we are!" They remind me so much of Samuel, whose story we are going to read next. Join me as I pick up the microphone to deliver the last lesson in the series Identity Crisis at Victory Tabernacle Pentecostal Church in Kingsport, Tennessee.

Part Three: Here I am

Let's go to 1 Samuel 3:

1 And the child Samuel ministered unto the Lord before Eli. And the word of the Lord was precious in those days; there was no open vision.

2 And it came to pass at that time, when Eli was laid down in his place, and his eyes began to wax dim, that he could not see;

3 And ere the lamp of God went out in the temple of the Lord, where the ark of God was, and Samuel was laid down to sleep;

4 That the Lord called Samuel: and he answered, Here am I.

5 And he ran unto Eli, and said, Here am I; for thou calledst me. And he said, I called not; lie down again. And he went and lay down.

6 And the Lord called yet again, Samuel. And Samuel arose and went to Eli, and said, Here am I; for thou didst call me. And he answered, I called not, my son; lie down again.

7 Now Samuel did not yet know the Lord, neither was the word of the Lord yet revealed unto him.

8 And the Lord called Samuel again the third time. And he arose and went to Eli, and said, Here am I;

for thou didst call me. And Eli perceived that the Lord had called the child.

9 Therefore Eli said unto Samuel, Go, lie down: and it shall be, if he call thee, that thou shalt say, Speak, Lord; for thy servant heareth. So Samuel went and lay down in his place.

10 And the Lord came, and stood, and called as at other times, Samuel, Samuel. Then Samuel answered, Speak; for thy servant heareth.

11 And the Lord said to Samuel, Behold, I will do a thing in Israel, at which both the ears of every one that heareth it shall tingle.

12 In that day I will perform against Eli all things which I have spoken concerning his house: when I begin, I will also make an end.

13 For I have told him that I will judge his house for ever for the iniquity which he knoweth; because his sons made themselves vile, and he restrained them not.

14 And therefore I have sworn unto the house of Eli, that the iniquity of Eli's house shall not be purged with sacrifice nor offering for ever.

15 And Samuel lay until the morning, and opened the doors of the house of the Lord. And Samuel feared to shew Eli the vision.

16 Then Eli called Samuel, and said, Samuel, my son. And he answered, Here am I. (KJV)

With the help of the Lord, I would like to teach the third message in our series. We've talked about "Who they say I am," we've talked about "Who I say I am," and now we are going to take Samuel's words and discuss the response God is looking for: "Here I am!"

Part of getting through an identity crisis is not only realizing who you are, but where you are. Once we understand that we are that royal priesthood called to show forth His praises, we should begin to be like Samuel in this scripture. Again and again in this chapter, Samuel makes himself available to the priest and to Jehovah. Frequently, he utters the phrase, "Here am I." He never hides from God. He never offers any excuses. He simply hears a voice and makes himself available. In fact, we learn that he, too, was a child, but unlike Jeremiah, he never says to Eli or to God, "Hey, I'm just a child. I'm too young for this. I can't do what you are asking me to do." Perhaps the fact that he was a child explains verse 7 that says he did not yet know the Lord and that God's word had yet been revealed to him.

I think it is interesting that verse 1 says he ministered to the Lord but verse 7 says he did not even know Him yet. As I read this scripture with fresh eyes for this August revival, I found that fact about Samuel odd, so I researched these verses a bit more closely. I discovered that Samuel ministered under the direction of Eli, but he did jobs such as opening the doors of the House of the Lord and other errands for Eli, the priest. We must remember that Eli and Samuel were living during a period of time when there was no great prophet on the scene. Samuel knew God, he worked in the house of the Lord, but he did not recognize God's voice. He did not initially understand how to operate as a prophet.

How many of you know that you can be busy in the house of the Lord but still not know Him in His fullness? Thank God that we can know more about Him, that we can grow in Him! No, we do not have to stay like children. A well-known preacher, John Gray, once said that it is possible to do the work of the Lord and forget the Lord of the work. Fortunately, Samuel did not do that. He was doing the work, and when God called him into a deeper anointing, into a deeper revelation, into a deeper relationship, the young boy did not say, "But I'm just a child!" He did not say "Opening the doors to the house of the Lord is enough," and he did not say, "I'm unable to go deeper with you Lord." He simply said three words that we would do well to learn: "Here am I!"

His response is even more impressive when we realize that God was calling Samuel to a particularly difficult task. In fact, the first prophecy that he was given was an indictment against Eli. Can you imagine how Samuel must have felt when he stood before the most significant adult in his life knowing that God was displeased with Eli and his sons? Verse 15 says that he was afraid, and I would say that fear ran deep. However, even though he was afraid to show the vision to Eli, in verse 16 Samuel still declares, "Here am I." Learning how to show up for God even when we have much to learn and even when we are afraid will go a long way in helping us solve any identity crisis we might have. If we can muster up the obedience and courage of Samuel, imagine what we might accomplish for God!

Stories of children scattered throughout the Bible teach imperative lessons. Long before Hannah prayed Samuel into existence, God promised Isaac to Abraham and Sarah. We know in Genesis 22 that God tested Abraham when Isaac was just a young boy. God kept His promise to Abraham by giving him this precious child, but then He commanded Abraham to sacrifice Isaac on an altar. The Bible does not record that Abraham ever argued with God or offered any excuses as to why he could not do the difficult task that God put before him. In fact, the conversation between Isaac and his father appears in Genesis 22:

7 And Isaac spake unto Abraham his father, and said, My father: and he said, Here am I, my son. And he said, Behold the fire and the wood: but where is the lamb for a burnt offering?

8 And Abraham said, My son, God will provide himself a lamb for a burnt offering: so they went both of them together.

9 And they came to the place which God had told him of; and Abraham built an altar there, and laid the wood in order, and bound Isaac his son, and laid him on the altar upon the wood.

10 And Abraham stretched forth his hand, and took the knife to slay his son.

11 And the angel of the Lord called unto him out of heaven, and said, Abraham, Abraham: and he said, Here am I. (KJV)

Abraham utters, "Here am I" three times in this chapter. Repeatedly, he responds to God in this affirmative, obedient way despite the fact that the Lord has given him the hardest, ugliest, most heartbreaking task of his life. Of course, God was not really going to require that Abraham sacrifice his son. We know from studying the Old Testament that the Lord did not condone child sacrifice, but Abraham did not know that. In the middle of his test, he uttered, "Here am I" not because He did not know God wouldn't really require him to go through with it, but because he knew his own identity. Abraham understood that he was a servant of the Most High. He also knew God as Jehovah-Jireh, God our Provider. I imagine that with each step he took, Abraham reminded himself that God could provide another sacrifice. My friends, when God requires the hard tasks from us, will we be brave enough and obedient enough to echo the voice of Abraham and Samuel? Will we declare, "Here am I"?

Consider what was required of our Savior. The story of Abraham and Isaac played out again on Golgotha's hill, but this time the Son would not be spared. Jesus was given the hardest assignment of eternity when He bore the cross. In John chapter 18 when His enemies came looking for our Messiah with torches and lanterns and weapons, Jesus asked them in verse 4 "Whom seek ye?" Here is the chilling exchange:

5 They answered him, Jesus of Nazareth. Jesus saith unto them, I am he. And Judas also, which betrayed him, stood with them.

6 As soon then as he had said unto them, I am he, they went backward, and fell to the ground.

7 Then asked he them again, Whom seek ye? And they said, Jesus of Nazareth.

8 Jesus answered, I have told you that I am he: if therefore ye seek me, let these go their way: (KJV, emphasis added)

The men were looking for Jesus. They wanted to know where He was. Jesus did not hesitate. In fact, three times the Lord said, "I am he." Jesus, who never had an identity crisis, in essence said, "I'm the one you are looking for. I'm standing right here. See? Here I am."

Friend, I do not think Jesus is ever going to ask you to do anything harder than what He did for us that night when He gave Himself to the authorities. Do you? If you answered no to that question, be available for Him.

REFLECTION:

1. In what ways can you make yourself available to God?

2. How do you tend to respond when God calls you to His service? Reflect on that answer.

The exchange between the preacher of the Word of God and the soul who says, “Here am I,” only happens when the bones of the mouth are willing to move. As you have probably guessed by now, I have done a little reading about the bones that make up the mouth. The lower jawbone is the mandible, and it is the strongest bone in the human face. God is not asking us to use something weak; He has endowed us with the strength we need to lift up His name even when circumstances might seem less than favorable.

Interestingly enough, below the mandible is one of the biggest mysteries of our anatomy: the chin. Would you believe that scientists are not sure why we have a chin? They have formed many theories, but studies have disproved most of those hypotheses. However, scientists are certain of one thing: Humans are the only species to have a chin! That’s right! We are set apart from all other living creatures because none of them have a chin. We are indeed a “peculiar people” chosen from among all created beings to show forth His praise. We do that when we engage the mandible and the chin to speak. Thus, we must learn to give God authority over our tongues, over our mouths. If we intend to start at the bone, the mouth seems to be our greatest prospect.

One theory regarding the chin presumes that it is a “spandrel.” That particular term is borrowed from architecture, which defines it as a “feature below some church domes that is often so ornate it looks as if it was the starting point for the building's design" (Hogenboom). However, careful examination of the dome will show that the spandrels "only exist because they help support the dome above them. In other words, spandrels–both biological and architectural–are a by-product of a change happening elsewhere." Noted biologists Stephen J. Gould and Richard Lewontin explain that chins are likewise the result "of a change happening elsewhere" (Hogenboom).

I think that is a lovely metaphor. What makes us distinctly human is the result of a change happening inside us. This change manifests as the infilling of the Holy Spirit when we engage all of the bones involved in producing sounds of praise–a distinctively human sound, for we are the only ones who can sing the song of the redeemed!

I am so thankful for every soul who answers the call to be available for God. I am thankful for each person who internalizes the preaching or teaching of God's word and determines in his or her heart to respond, "Here am I, Lord. Send me."

Covenant with God is a beautiful thing. Partnership with Him is peaceful. Is He calling you to greater works of obedience? Is He asking you to trust Him with something or someone you treasure infinitely? Step out into the water. Come like a child. Eager. Enthusiastic. Willing. See if He does not make Myranda's favorite verse-Jeremiah 29:11- your reality.

Baptismal service at Manville Holiness Church.
My sons, Andrew and Tim, assist as my father looks on.
Casey Tanner and Myranda are all smiles with me on the bridge.

Chapter Five

Ride His Shoulder

I am the good shepherd. The good shepherd lays down his life for the sheep-John 10:11 (ESV)

Have you ever noticed that you can read certain scriptures repeatedly and not grasp their unique significance until God sees fit to put it in your line of vision? I remember distinctly when Luke 15: 4-7 came into unique focus for me. The text offers these words of Jesus:

4 "What man of you, having a hundred sheep, if he loses one of them, does not leave the ninety-nine in the wilderness, and go after the one which is lost until he finds it?

5 And when he has found it, he lays it on his shoulders, rejoicing.

6 And when he comes home, he calls together his friends and neighbors, saying to them, 'Rejoice with me, for I have found my sheep which was lost!'

7 I say to you that likewise there will be more joy in heaven over one sinner who repents than over ninety-nine just persons who need no repentance." (NKJV)

I had immersed myself in Lysa TerKeurst's Bible Study, *Finding I Am*, (which I highly recommend, by the way) when God's time and vision lined up for me. A description in Luke 15:5 captivated me, and I would like to call that image to your attention: ***He lays it on His shoulders, rejoicing***. That image was not the focus of *Finding I Am*, but somehow it fascinated me. As I began looking into it, that scripture revealed a beautiful truth to me about Jesus and His identity as our shepherd.

In the last chapter, I discussed the fact that Jesus never had an identity crisis. He knew exactly who He was and exactly why He had come to dwell among His flock. We only have to look to His Word to understand the dimensions of His identity. He is the bread of life come down from heaven as the babe swaddled in the manger. He is the way, the truth, and the life. He is the light and the resurrection. He is the Word wrapped in flesh. He is the fullness of the Godhead appearing in bodily form (Colossians 2:9). He is all of these things and more!

Because He knew His identity as the Logos of God (John 1:1-14), He was able to defeat Satan in the wilderness by proclaiming the Word of God (Luke and Matthew 4). Because He understood that He is Alpha and Omega, He was able to tell the thief on the cross, "This day, thou shalt see Me in Paradise." When He declared, "It is finished," He knew that He was not. Because He accepted His divine role as the Good Shepherd, He has always been able to shoulder His sheep.

Join me in Manville, as I discuss God's identity as the Good Shepherd, the Shepherd whose voice we know, in the next sermon entitled "Shouldering the Sheep."

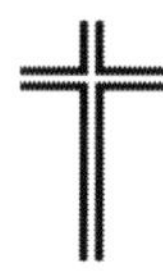

When I really began to focus on the shepherd's description in Luke 15:5, I did a little research and as often happens with stories from the Bible, several well-meaning myths popped up. We have to be careful as we separate fact from fiction when we are mining the Word of God. I find that many myths, in fact, have been circulated about eagles and sheep that just are not true. They sound good. They teach a moral. However, they are false and unnecessary. God's scriptures do not need any fiction to help them. His Word is powerful all by itself.

The myth surrounding this text from Luke went something like this: If a sheep keeps wandering off, the Shepherd will break one of its legs when he finds it, thus forcing the herdsman to carry the bleating, injured, pitiful creature home on his shoulders. That just didn't sit right with me. To me, that was more about punishment and control than comforting and guiding. I couldn't imagine a shepherd rejoicing after having to break his sheep's leg. Sure enough, a little further study revealed to me that this story wasn't true at all.

My friends in Virginia who have raised animals know that no farmer, no shepherd, would ever do such a thing. They will tell you that breaking an animal's leg is risky and can end in trauma. The animal will most likely not sell and will cost the farmer some money. Clearly, the myth is false, but the truth is quite beautiful. Here is what really happens:

The loving shepherd hoists the lamb onto his shoulder and carries it home because the animal has worn itself out. Fatigued and perhaps injured from its own actions, the bewildered animal is most likely terrified. It bleats, and the Good Shepherd hears and rescues it. Now that is cause for celebration, not the brutal breaking of a wayward animal's limbs!

Nothing in this scripture remotely suggests that the shepherd breaks any of the sheep's bones. Satisfied that I understood the mythology around this story, I had to keep searching to figure out why I was so captivated by the phrase "laying it on his shoulders." Let me share with you what I found out.

In John 10:14, Jesus said that He is the Good Shepherd who gives His life for the sheep. A shepherd in Jesus' day did not use dogs that would bark loudly and nip at the sheep to get them to move out of panic or pain. I have news for pastors today. They shouldn't either. In Jesus' lifetime, shepherding looked much different. In fact, the shepherd took every effort to make sure that the sheep were safe and without blemish. He would often put himself in danger simply to protect the sheep; as a result, the sheep learned to trust his voice and respond to it. In fact, according to Lysa TerKeurst, multiple families kept their sheep in the same sheep gate. How did they separate and gather them? Each flock knew its particular shepherd's voice just as we know the Good Shepherd's voice. Thank God for a shepherd whose voice we can recognize and who lays us on His shoulder when we have worn ourselves out trying to find our own way–when we have injured ourselves from bad choices and bad direction!

I would imagine that all of us could sympathize with that sheep who somehow managed to get itself lost. Something perhaps drew it off course; it wandered too long or too fast and lost the rest of the group. At some point, it had to notice, "Hey! Where are all of the other sheep?" The trick of the enemy is to keep you out there once you are isolated, once you have made a mistake, once you have somehow gotten off track. The lost sheep is probably listening for a voice, and if the shepherd seems far away, the animal might become hopeless.

Ever do that? Ever find yourself wandering off course? Before you know it, you are utterly isolated and you begin to think to yourself, "If I could just hear the voice of my God, I know that I would be saved!"

We might suppose that as soon as that sheep heard the voice of the Good Shepherd, it would come bounding to him. However, if we look back at Luke's text, verse 5 says that the shepherd has found it, gone to it, and lifted it up onto his shoulder. The only thing that the sheep did right in this scenario was not running away from its master. We are stubborn creatures, are we not? When we have managed to separate ourselves from the voice of God, we hesitate to run back to Him when we hear His call. We tell ourselves that He is going to be angry. Maybe we have bought into the myth that He only wants to break us. What a mistake!

When God starts pulling at your heart, when God starts dealing with you right where you are, do not run from

Him. Do not be afraid to ride His shoulder because that is what He wants you to do. Maybe you just need to let Him carry you for a while. Don't run. Don't be afraid. He isn't going to break your bones. He just wants to start at the bone. He just wants to pick you up and carry you out of your mistake. Out of your miscalculation. Out of your regret. Out of your heartbreak. Out of your addiction. Your sin. Your isolation.

How do I know that God's shoulder is designed for that? Consider Isaiah 9:6:

For unto us a child is born, unto us a son is given, and the government shall be upon his shoulder: and his name shall be called Wonderful, Counsellor, the mighty god, the everlasting Father, the Prince of Peace. (KJV, emphasis added)

The Hebrew word for shoulder in this verse means "place of burdens." According to Strong's Bible Concordance, it carries the connotation of "shouldering a blow, bearing up, and bearing as a burden." Figuratively, the word means "the spur of the hill." I want you to internalize that image for a moment.

What made Jesus move from being the Lamb of God to operating as our Shepherd? What took place in His life that elevated Him from sacrificial lamb to the Good Shepherd? Did it not begin at the place of the skull, at the place of burdens? Did it not begin at the spur of Calvary's hill?

I want you to get a mental image of this transition for a moment. Before God found you, picked you up, and laid you on His shoulder, what did He carry on that same shoulder? My friends, it was the beam of the cross. Isaiah proclaimed that the government would be upon His shoulder, and the entire weight of the government certainly rode His shoulders all the way up Golgotha!

Why was He willing to do that? The answer is profound. He did it so that you could eventually ride upon His shoulder–a place of strength. Isaiah 46:4 declares, "Even to your old age I am he: and even to your white hair will I carry you: I have made, and I will bear; even I will carry, and will deliver you." What a Savior we serve!

No, my friends, He doesn't break your legs. He doesn't crush your bones. Instead, He will protect and love you. I am not saying bad things will never happen, and I am not saying the Lord does not chastise. He does. However, when it comes to the work of salvation, He took that upon His shoulder because He loves you and rejoices in you.

Consider what He endured before He arrived at the spur of the hill. Matthew 27:28-29 records:

28 And they stripped Him and put a scarlet robe on Him.

29 When they had twisted a crown of thorns, they put it on His head, and a reed in His right hand. And they bowed the knee before Him and mocked Him, saying, "Hail, King of the Jews!" (NKJV)

Please do not overlook that crown of thorns because it contains a powerful truth when we consider this teaching from TerKeurst's *Finding I Am*. She writes, "Overnight the sheep were placed in roughly constructed round stone-walled enclosures. The top of the wall was covered with thorns to keep the wild animals out" (77, emphasis added). Can we not see Christ in this description? At the top of His head and at the top of the sheep enclosure, we find thorns. His thorny crown signifies His protection over you–His desire to keep things that would devour you far from you.

TerKeurst goes on to write, "Inside the enclosure the sheep were safe so long as the entrance was secured by the shepherd. He slept across the entrance as there was no door" (77). Friends, as long as He is there, we have a door. His word proclaims that He is the door to the sheep (John 10:7). If you get out of the sheepfold, if you wander off and get lost, He will come looking for you and carry you back where you belong. Do you know what He will do for you next? Get excited! Because His provision is remarkable!

When you rest and become stronger, He will transition you to greater works. I want you to notice something about the beam that was upon His shoulder. Matthew 27:30-32 records:

30 Then they spat on Him, and took the reed and struck Him on the head.

31 And when they had mocked Him, they took the robe off Him, put His own clothes on Him, and led Him away to be crucified.

32 Now as they came out, they found a man of Cyrene, Simon by name. Him they compelled to bear His cross. (NKJV)

We all know Jesus was God in the flesh, so why did He have to have help here? The whole government up until that point had been on His shoulder. He is strong enough to shoulder anything. Why did he need Simon?

We have to understand that He is teaching us our part in His kingdom's work. Verse 32 points out that Jesus handed the work of salvation, the work of the cross, over to humanity. We are to continue lifting one another up, bearing one another's burdens. We are to become strength for those who have none. We are to point them to the Good Shepherd. In this regard, shoulder moves from a noun to a verb.

Matthew Henry's commentary states that the word "shoulder" denotes power. What were the disciples waiting for in the Upper Room as recorded in Acts 2? Christ had told them to tarry in Jerusalem until they received power from on high! Power to do what? To shoulder the work of Christ! To live an overcoming life so that they could shoulder the work of the cross. Pastors are called shepherds, in fact, because it is their job to shoulder the sheep. If you do not have a good pastor in your life, you need one. You need a Simon of Cyrene. Someone who has grasped the work of the cross with willing hands.

You see, there is a reason that Christ transformed Peter, a fisherman, into a shepherd who could feed his sheep. In Peter's day, the fishermen caught the fish and immediately separated them out according to what the catch could do for them. A fisherman might say, "This one is in. It's big enough and can bring me wages. This one is too little and will cost more in taxes than it is worth. I have to toss it out."

Being a shepherd requires a completely different mindset. Good shepherds do not toss people aside after sizing them up.

Even if you are not a pastor, there is ministry in your life. The Apostle Paul instructed us to take heed to the ministry entrusted to us that we might fulfill it. Ride His shoulder when you need to, but put your shoulder into whatever He has given you to do.

We know that sheep wander off. We know that they get lost. Another peculiarity about sheep is their poor eyesight. Every now and then, it is good for them to rest and let the Shepherd carry them on His shoulder where they can see things a little more clearly. Do not run from your time on His shoulder. Let him be the God of Isaiah 46. But know this: His Word is a lamp unto your feet, so eventually you will have to walk again. If Simon of Cyrene could take up that cross behind Him, what is to keep us from doing the same?

When I first began to write this book, I selected the most recent sermons that I had delivered because that just made sense to me. One day, I was looking for a particular sermon and found the one that you just read. I pulled it aside thinking, "I might need this one." Shouldering the Sheep was preached several years ago, and at first when I pulled it from my notebook, the fact that it had an actual bone in the title didn't even occur to me! Now, as I sit in front of my computer on a rainy day in April, I realize why God prompted me to select this particular message that had been stuffed into my minister's notebook about four years ago.

A quick Google search of shoulder anatomy reveals these truths about the shoulder. First, the shoulder is one of the "largest and most complex joints in the body." The shoulder joint is "formed where the humerus...fits into the scapula...like a ball and socket" (Hoffman). That reminds me of Jesus' teaching about God's husbandry. In John 15, did He not say, "I am the vine and ye are the branches"? In order for the branches to live, they must be connected to the vine. Likewise, in order for the shoulder to work, the humerus bone must be connected to the scapula. However, it is more complicated than that. Other bones make up the complex shoulder joint including the acromion, the clavicle, and the coracoid process. If any of these bones separate from the scapula, serious pain ensues. Catch that! Pain ensues!

The irony of the shoulder's anatomy is that the humerus fits loosely into the shoulder joint, giving it "a wide range of motion" while rendering it "vulnerable to injury" (Hoffman). One of the most common shoulder injuries results from the separation or dislocation of the bones from the joint. When the humerus or one of the other bones in the shoulder slips out of position, raising the arm will cause pain and a popping sensation (Hoffman). Other afflictions also result when any of the structures that make up the shoulder sustain injury: the rotator cuff, the bursa, and the labrum.

Can we consider this complex bone structure as a living metaphor of the Church? The Church is indeed a large and complex structure made of many moving parts. When any of those parts separate from the main joint, excruciating pain results. It is important that connection exist and that separated members are restored so that the Church can function in its wide range of motion. After all, its range had better be far reaching, as the Gospel of Jesus Christ must be carried to all nations and tongues. The infrastructure of the Church must be healthy and functioning, and all of its distinct parts must perform optimally if the whole world is to come to the knowledge of Christ.

How does a doctor repair a dislocation? How does the doctor ensure that the patient will regain his or her range of motion? He or she almost always starts with the bone. In fact, when the doctor is able to put the bone back in its proper place, the pain relief is usually immediate.

Are you hurting today? Do you feel disconnected? Separated? Do you need to be restored to your proper place in God? He is able to shoulder you. Let Him start at the place where you first lost connection. Don't run from Him. Let Him find you. Let Him start at the bone.

REFLECTION:

1. Are there any points of separation in your life that need to be repaired?

2. How can you yield to God's healing of that separation?

3. Are there any points of separation in your church that need to be repaired?

4. Do you have any role beyond prayer in healing any church separations? If so, what steps can you take?

Chapter Six

Listen to God Sing

"For God so loved the world, that he gave his only begotten Son, that whosoever believeth in him should not perish, but have everlasting life."-John 3:16 KJV

One of my favorite worship songs of all time is "Reckless Love" which showcases the genius songwriting talents of Cory Asbury, Caleb Culver, and Ran Jackson. The lyrics recount the story of the Good Shepherd that I discussed in chapter 5, stating that there is no mountain that God won't climb up to find the wayward sheep. The chorus cries that the reckless love of God "Chases me down! Fights till I'm found! Leaves the 99!"

Yes, in what seems like a reckless venture, the Shepherd leaves 99 secured sheep and goes to rescue the lost one. He goes no matter what. No matter the weather. No matter the terrain. No matter the climb. However, knowing what we know about the Good Shepherd (and understanding that we all have to ride His shoulder from time to time), we realize that His actions are not foolish at all. The 99 sheep will remain safe because according to Jesus, His sheep listen to His voice. He gives them eternal life and "they shall never perish; no one will snatch them out of [His] hand" (John 10:28, *NIV*). Do not miss that truth: A key to eternal life is listening to God.

Another beautiful image in "Reckless Love" recounts God singing over His creation. Cory acknowledges God's love for humanity with an image from the Old Testament: "Before I took a breath, You were singing over me." Although I loved this lyrical line the first time I heard it, I never really understood its significance until I did a deeper study of the little book of poetry from the minor prophet Zephaniah. The Bible is so rich, so full, so intricate, and so powerful, that I could live to be 100 and still not scratch the surface. I have much to learn about the Minor Prophets, but Zephaniah taught me how much God really does love us–and that was what Cory was singing about all along!

Can we just stop our busy world right now? Just hit pause. Wherever you are, whatever you are doing, I encourage you to stop for just a moment, and receive the love of God. Push the play button on "Reckless Love," or your favorite worship song, and just spend some time listening to lyrics that celebrate God's love. I'm serious. Do it.

Listen.

Breathe.

Tell the Lord you love Him.

Tell the Lord you receive His love for you.

Now, don't you feel better? Something about worship just lifts our spirits! Whether you can sing like a professional or can't carry a tune in a bucket, God loves to hear you sing. In fact, the Bible says, "Make a joyful noise!" It doesn't say it has to be beautiful!

Yes, God loves to hear you sing, but did you know that He sings, too? According to Zephaniah, you are commanded to sing unto God, and God rejoices over you in loud singing! That's right! YOU make God break out in song! If you look at the chapters of Zephaniah's book in the ESV or any other comparable translation, you will see that it is indeed written as poetry. In fact, many prophets wrote in verse. Given the fact that almost 35% of the Bible is poetry, I suppose I shouldn't have been surprised to discover that God is a lyricist and a singer. What is most shocking to me, though, is that He wants to rejoice over me! Over you! Over His creation! For God so loved the world that He sang over it!

I want you to enjoy the beautiful poetry of Zephaniah for a moment. I have arranged chapter 3:8-20 (ESV) on one page for you to take in. Pay particular attention to the verse I put in bold print for you.

Then meet me on the page that follows Zephaniah's poem for the sermon, "The God Who Sings."

__8__ "Therefore wait for me," declares the Lord, "for the day when I rise up to seize the prey.

For my decision is to gather nations, to assemble kingdoms,to pour out upon them my indignation, all my burning anger;

for in the fire of my jealousy all the earth shall be consumed.

__9__ "For at that time I will change the speech of the peoples to a pure speech, that all of them may call upon the name of the Lord and serve him with one accord.

__10__ From beyond the rivers of Cush my worshipers, the daughter of my dispersed ones, shall bring my offering.

__11__ "On that day you shall not be put to shame because of the deeds by which you have rebelled against me;

for then I will remove from your midst your proudly exultant ones,and you shall no longer be haughty in my holy mountain.

__12__ But I will leave in your midst a people humble and lowly.

They shall seek refuge in the name of the Lord,

__13__ those who are left in Israel;they shall do no injustice

and speak no lies,nor shall there be found in their mouth a deceitful tongue.

For they shall graze and lie down, and none shall make them afraid."

__14__ Sing aloud, O daughter of Zion; shout, O Israel!

Rejoice and exult with all your heart, O daughter of Jerusalem!

__15__ The Lord has taken away the judgments against you; he has cleared away your enemies.

The King of Israel, the Lord, is in your midst; you shall never again fear evil.

__16__ On that day it shall be said to Jerusalem:

"Fear not, O Zion let not your hands grow weak.

17 The Lord your God is in your midst,

a mighty one who will save;

he will rejoice over you with gladness;

he will quiet you by his love;

he will exult over you with loud singing.

__18__ I will gather those of you who mourn for the festival so that you will no longer suffer reproach.[a]

__19__ Behold, at that time I will deal with all your oppressors. And I will save the lame and gather the outcast,

and I will change their shame into praise and renown in all the earth.

__20__ At that time I will bring you in,at the time when I gather you together;

for I will make you renowned and praised among all the peoples of the earth, when I restore your fortunes before your eyes," says the Lord.

You might have cringed when I told you to turn to Zephaniah. You might have felt a spirit of angst rise up in you as I directed you to one of the prophets of the Old Testament. I can understand why. After all, the prophets often came preaching death, destruction, justice, and judgment; to be sure, Zephaniah is no different.

The Book of Zephaniah is divided into three sections. In the first section of the book, we see a reversal of the ordered world that God created in the Book of Genesis. Everything has shifted under the weight of human sin and chaos, and Zephaniah warns his people that God is going to send an army to wipe them out (Mackie and Collins). In fact, the first section is all about God's judgment on Judah and Jerusalem for its corruption and its idolatry. The second section is all about God's judgment on ALL of the nations, and Zephaniah again calls Jerusalem by name. (Mackie and Collins). The last section is our scripture text for today: Zephaniah 3:8-20.

I want you to notice what God does. In essence, He says, "I've made a decision. I'm going to send a fire." We all know the destructive power of fire. In fact, in Amos chapter 2 verse 2, Amos prophesies that the Lord will "send a fire upon Moab and it shall devour their palaces and Moab shall die with tumult, with shouting, and with the sound of the trumpet." Sounds a whole lot like justice to me.

Zephaniah's approach, however, differs from Amos' approach. Zephaniah presents the two characteristics of God that tell the whole story. He discusses God's justice and God's love (Mackie and Collins). The justice might sound scary to us, as verse 8 declares God intends "to gather nations, to assemble kingdoms, to pour out upon them my indignation, all my burning anger; for in the fire of my jealousy all the earth shall be consumed." This fire, though, contrasts Amos' prophesied inferno. God's shifting voice in verse 9 reveals the contrast as the Lord declares, "For at that time I will change the speech of the peoples to a pure speech, that all of them may call upon the name of the Lord and serve him with one accord." Sounds a whole lot like restoration to me.

This third section of Zephaniah goes on to tell how the Lord's fire will restore hope to EVERYONE. Here are just a few groups that are included as "everyone": sinners, backsliders, the poor, the needy, the afflicted, the outcasts! Conversely, God says those who have been prideful, driving out the marginalized groups, will be cast out themselves (Zephaniah 3:11-12). You see, God's ways are not our ways. He removes those who think they are exalted, but He leaves among us the discounted, the poor, and the afflicted. Why? Because they trust the Lord. Isn't that remarkable? Is it true? All we have to do to remain in the midst of those marked for restoration is trust the Lord? Yes–trust and praise Him. He demands that His people sing the songs of Zion.

How is God going to pull this off? How is He going to bring all of the outcasts, the afflicted, and the poor out from under justice and into His love? The key is verse 9. Zephaniah sees God's fire coming toward Jerusalem to turn the people "toward a pure language." This fire is not a destructive inferno; rather, it is a purifying flame. On the Day of Pentecost, in Acts chapter 2, the fire settled upon Jesus' disciples as "cloven tongues of fire." It descended upon Jerusalem that day, and just as pure language promotes unity, it bonded 3,000 of them in a baptismal experience: the same experience that John the Baptist prophesied when he said that one greater than himself was coming to "baptize you with Holy Ghost and fire" (Matthew 3:11).

Centuries before John the Baptist emerged from the wilderness preparing the way of the Lord, Zephaniah was prophesying the purifying fire and unifying language of the Holy Ghost! Zephaniah, like Joel, was prophesying the outpouring of the Holy Spirit, which began in Jerusalem and spread all over the world much like a fire that cannot be contained. Zephaniah knew that the Holy Ghost fire would purify the Jewish people.

It will purify you, too. If you've been driven out, God says you are welcome in His kingdom. If you are facing or have faced poverty, He says, "Enter in." If you are sick and afflicted, God says, "Let my fire purify you." The day of Pentecost is fully here. In the end, Zephaniah's prophecy did not only deal with the dispersed Jews. He saw much further into God's plan than that. The message is clear: God wants to restore ALL of us!

What should we do once we receive His purifying Spirit? What does He call us to do? According to this prophecy, we must stop being afraid, and we must start doing God's work. The prophet tells us not to let our hands be slack. Get busy with your calling! Praise Him in your busyness!

If you think for one moment that God does not see you, that God does not care about you, that God does not love you, consider my favorite verse in this whole chapter. Verse 17. He loves you. So much in fact, that He sings over you. I know we are accustomed to praising Him in song, but did you ever for one moment think of God singing because of YOU? Even if you are depressed and driven out, you are forlorn and weary, or you are unpolished and cast aside, you are just what He is looking for (Zephaniah 3:18-19). The scripture doesn't say He sings over the proud. It doesn't say that He rejoices over the polished. He sings over those of us who are poor, afflicted, wounded, and broken. If you have been talked about and cast out, He has a song for you!

In the Book of Amos, the trumpet signals destruction, but Zephaniah brings a message of hope. I'd like for us to consider a different trumpet. Read Revelation 1:10 from the NIV:

On the Lord's Day I was in the Spirit, and I heard behind me a loud voice like a trumpet.

This trumpeting sound differs from the one we hear in Amos' prophecy. John the Revelator hears God singing again, and His voice is great like a trumpet's music. John looks to see who is beckoning to him and describes one "like the Son of Man":

14 The hair on his head was white like wool, as white as snow, and his eyes were like blazing fire.

15 His feet were like bronze glowing in a furnace, and his voice was like the sound of rushing waters.

This description is astounding. I would like to focus first on the simile that compares God's voice to the sound of rushing waters. Dan Parilis, a singer and voice teacher, says that the difference in speaking and singing is simply flow. What flows more than many waters coming together? I can think of nothing. The flow of God's voice, like the sound of rushing waters, tells me that our God, like in Zephaniah's prophecy, is singing yet again!

That is not the only similarity between John's vision and Zephaniah's. Look at John's description of God's eyes. They are like fire! Revelation 1 points to Zephaniah's prophecy repeatedly. The purifying fire of Zephaniah 3:8 has come, and God is singing with the voice of many waters and the sound of a trumpet. I don't know about you, but the description of God in verses 14 and 15 intimidates me. John was obviously intimidated as well, but the Lord commands him not to fear. The Revelator writes in verse 17:

When I saw him, I fell at his feet as though dead. Then he placed his right hand on me and said: "Do not be afraid. I am the First and the Last."

The first thing that God says to John is "Do not be afraid!" I worry that the Church's biggest obstacle today is fear. I know beyond a shadow of a doubt that fear is my biggest problem. My inner dialogue often sounds like this:

"What if this doesn't work?"

"What is going to happen next?"

"What if I fail?"

"What if I'm not good enough?"

"What if people don't approve of my calling?"

All these "what ifs" could go on forever if I do not learn to stand up to my fear. I wear myself out with this clandestine conversation, and I venture to guess that you have asked yourself similar questions before, too. We hinder ourselves with our fear and doubt when all the while God loves us and just wants to rejoice with us in singing. We know we want to hear that God song! How can we make Him sing?

First of all, we must trust Him. Second, we must sing praises unto Him. In fact, Zephaniah tells us that the Lord called His people into hope, shouting, "Sing O daughters of Zion!" Third, we have to stop being afraid of everything. When we receive clear direction, we cannot be slack which leads me to the fourth point: We cannot faint! We must be all that God has called us to be, but many of us refuse to do that because we do not see ourselves as someone that God loves enough to sing about.

Think about it. The Creator, with a voice as of the sound of many waters, the One who holds the whole world in His hand, is moved to sing for YOU. Do you believe that He can love you like that? Do you think you have fallen short too often? Perhaps you need to consider Zephaniah's people. After all, they were worshipping other gods; they had completely fallen away from God; they had abused His love time and time again. Still, He said, "I'm going to call you back to Me. I'm going to restore you. I'm going to rejoice over you in singing!"

We simply cannot be afraid to do what God has called us to do. Let me tell you a story about how fear works. Remember the prophet Jeremiah? I'm willing to bet that you have heard quite a bit about him. Have you heard of the prophet Urijah, though? He is a little less well known. However, Jeremiah and Urijah were contemporaries, both preaching and prophesying God's word at the same time. You see, God gave them each the same prophecy, but only Jeremiah was brave enough to deliver it. He boldly conveyed an unpopular and unwelcome message to an earthly king. He knew the king would not graciously receive his message, but he still delivered it. Not Urijah. He was fearful. He lost trust in the God who sings. Sadly, the Bible records that he fled to Egypt where the king's soldiers hunted him down, killed him, and threw him into a common grave. You can find his tragedy in Jeremiah 26. His story is not the story I want for God's Church. I do not want us to be so slack, so afraid, so untrusting, that we run from God and miss His singing.

A few centuries ago, the famous composer, Ludwig van Beethoven, used bone conduction to continue composing music after his auditory nerve was damaged. Later in his life, he was almost completely deaf, but he learned to hear the sound of the piano by using his jawbone! Sounds incredible, doesn't it? Nevertheless, that is exactly what he did. He would attach a rod to his piano and clench it in his teeth, and the piano's sound vibrations would "transfer from the piano to his jaw" ("Bone Conduction"). His musical genius did more than give us beautiful compositions; it proved "that sound could reach our auditory system through another medium besides eardrums, and the other medium is our bones" ("Bone Conduction").

I'm forever grateful to Beethoven because in December of 2019, I gained a beautiful, intelligent, deaf daughter-in-law who hears via cochlear implant. Bethany, my oldest son's beautiful bride, hears through bone conduction like Beethoven. She does not consider herself disabled and does not think she needs to be healed although some well-meaning, uninformed people might suggest that. Why? Because she hears a different way! She starts at the bone!

Might I suggest that if we want to learn the art of listening to God, we need to be like Bethany? We need to hear Him with our whole being. We need to hear His commands as vibrations conducted throughout our whole body. We need to hear and respond. The prophet Jeremiah heard God's voice and wanted to run rather than respond, but he soon realized that God's command was like "fire shut up in [his] bones" (Jeremiah 20:9). Am I suggesting that you are going to hear an audible voice from God? No–although I certainly believe that can happen. I am suggesting to you that hearing God's voice moves beyond hearing. Just as with sound waves, we do not merely hear God, we feel Him.

How can that be? Consider the eardrum. It consists of three bones: the malleus, the incus, and the stapes. The head of the malleus and the body of the incus "are held together by a tightly fitting joint... seated in the attic, or upper portion, of the eardrum cavity" ("Ear Bones"). These bones respond to normal sound waves that are actually tiny vibrations in the air. Once these vibrations hit our ears, the eardrum actually decodes the sound waves and sends them to the cochlea, which transmits the sound to the brain ("Bone Conduction"). If the auditory nerve does not work properly, bone conduction can serve as an alternative receiver of sound. The bone conduction device, such as a cochlear implant or Beethoven's rod, bypasses the defective eardrum allowing sound to reach "the ears as vibrations through the bones (or skull) and skin" ("Bone Conduction").

Sometimes to hear from God, you have to start at the bone that will work, and we have to understand that all of us have unique ways of communicating with the Lord.

Let me explain the analogy here. Just as the bones of the eardrum are held together by a joint and seated in the attic of the eardrum cavity, the disciples were held together by their belief in Christ and gathered in the attic or upper room. The first stimulus that they responded to was sound. The Book of Acts records that they heard a sound from heaven as of a rushing mighty wind. This sequence makes sense when we remember that normal sound waves travel as vibrations through the air or wind. First, they heard God! Next, their sight was engaged, and they saw cloven tongues like fire. Finally, they began to speak as the spirit "gave utterance."

My point is that we need to learn to **feel** God's voice as the upper room attendees did. John's experience on the Isle of Patmos, in fact, mirrors the upper room event. He hears God, he sees God's prophecies, and then he speaks. We find this pattern in the first chapter of Revelation. God told John to hear what the Spirit was saying to the churches, but John didn't just **hear**. In fact, John declared that during his banishment to Patmos, he was "in the Spirit." He first felt God, and then he heard God's trumpet-like voice. Finally, God began to reveal the visions that He destined John to share. Would any of that have mattered if John hadn't been caught up "in the Spirit on the Lord's Day" as recorded in Revelation 1: 10? Sometimes we have to stop relying on our humanity–the parts of us that do not function properly–and just yield to His Spirit like the 120 in the upper chamber and John at Patmos. Let's learn to bypass our humanity and get in tune with God. We need to have that upper room experience for ourselves. When we do that, we can hear Him sing.

Like a loving mother wrapping her arms around her newborn babe, holding the little one to her heart, and singing a glad lullaby, God will gather you unto Himself. He will sing loudly with great rejoicing because you have found your way to your Father! Let Him permeate your whole being. Get caught up in His Spirit and listen. Listen to Him sing.

REFLECTION:

1. How do you commune with God?

2. What obstacles hinder your communication with God? How can you work around them?

3. Read Acts 2. Identify the most striking moments of the narrative.

4. What would "an upper room experience" look like to you in your life? In your church?

Chapter Seven

Look up!

"The eye is the lamp of the body; so then if your eye is clear, your whole body will be full of light- Matthew 6:22 (NASB)

Easter 2020 was approaching, and I was scheduled to speak in Manville. Bringing the Easter message is both an honor and delight, but 2020 was throwing all sense of normalcy out of the window. I would be delivering the Easter message all right, but I would have to do it via YouTube as Covid-19 had shut down houses of worship everywhere.

Even as I sit writing this chapter at the close of April 2020, Covid-19 is still with us. My home state, Tennessee, has entered Phase 1 of reopening after Governor William "Bill" Lee issued shelter in place mandates a few weeks ago. Prior to Phase 1, the government allowed churches to hold services as long as only 10 people attended; of course, that stipulation made carrying on as usual completely out of the question. The month of April saw pastors arrested and churchgoers fined as clergy turned to the internet to offer their congregations online sermons. Learning to use wisdom in the face of a threatening virus has been the order of the day. It will be interesting to read about this pandemic in a few years: how it changed the world, our churches, and us. Yes, it will be interesting to see how 2020 goes down in history.

Given the frenzied nature of our world right now, I am not surprised that many students of the Bible are quoting Chronicles these days. Listen to the promise and its condition in 2 Chronicles 7:14:

"If my people, which are called by my name, shall humble themselves, and pray, and seek my face, and turn from their wicked ways; then will I hear from heaven, and will forgive their sin, and will heal their land." (KJV)

Healing. Truly what our nation desires. But to whom or what will we look for that healing? Whom will we trust? As Easter 2020 approached, I wanted to answer those questions while still commemorating the resurrection of our Lord.

Somewhere in cyberspace there is a video of me discussing a sickness, a curse if you will, in Moses' day. It might seem odd that I would teach an Easter message by starting in the Book of Numbers, but in that story we see a leader who advocates for the healing of his people, that same sort of cry that the Lord's voice describes in 2 Chronicles. It is a story of human frailty, divine healing, and Master plans. In the end, it is another story of bones. Listen in as I teach, "The Bone Box."

Let's begin by reading Numbers 21: 1-9

21 And when king Arad the Canaanite, which dwelt in the south, heard tell that Israel came by the way of the spies; then he fought against Israel, and took some of them prisoners.

2 And Israel vowed a vow unto the Lord, and said, If thou wilt indeed deliver this people into my hand, then I will utterly destroy their cities.

3 And the Lord hearkened to the voice of Israel, and delivered up the Canaanites; and they utterly destroyed them and their cities: and he called the name of the place Hormah.

4 And they journeyed from mount Hor by the way of the Red sea, to compass the land of Edom: and the soul of the people was much discouraged because of the way.

5 And the people spake against God, and against Moses, Wherefore have ye brought us up out of Egypt to die in the wilderness? for there is no bread, neither is there any water; and our soul loatheth this light bread.

6 And the Lord sent fiery serpents among the people, and they bit the people; and much people of Israel died.

7 Therefore the people came to Moses, and said, We have sinned, for we have spoken against the Lord, and against thee; pray unto the Lord, that he take away the serpents from us. And Moses prayed for the people.

8 And the Lord said unto Moses, Make thee a fiery serpent, and set it upon a pole: and it shall come to pass, that every one that is bitten, when he looketh upon it, shall live.

9 And Moses made a serpent of brass, and put it upon a pole, and it came to pass, that if a serpent had bitten any man, when he beheld the serpent of brass, he lived. (KJV)

On Easter Sunday, I know everyone expects us to read from the New Testament, and I promise that I am going to get there. However, before I do, I want us to see the design pattern of salvation. This scripture from Numbers also highlights the frailty of human nature: the whole reason we need God in the first place.

Interestingly enough, this text actually begins with a victory. The people cry out to the Lord and He delivers them. Immediately after their deliverance, though, the people begin to complain. Here we see a pattern all too common with humanity: ingratitude sets it, it combines with discouragement, and the result is sin. Here we have a people who have just experienced an awesome victory because God moved on their behalf, but verse 4 reveals that the people were "discouraged because of the way." When their traveling becomes difficult, they begin to speak against God and Moses. Punishment then comes in the form of fiery serpents, which, of course, gets their attention.

Realizing that they have sinned, the Israelites go to Moses and admit their wrongdoing. I know Moses was not a perfect man, but his actions in this story are honorable. Notice that the people tell him that they have spoken against him. They admit they have wronged him; however, instead of holding any sort of grudge, Moses seeks God's mercy on their behalf. What leadership! Despite their betrayal, Moses pleads with God to deliver them. This deliverance, of course, depicts the ancient pattern of salvation that we are still enjoying today.

God is moved by their admission of guilt, but He does not remove the source of punishment. Instead, He institutes salvation based upon obedience. The fiery serpents could still bite them, but if the Hebrews would focus on God's ordinance, if they would look upon the bronze statue instead of complaining in their discouragement, the serpent's bite could have no effect.

Fast forward 2,000 years and we have another instance in which Satan and death have no sting–no victory–because God resurrects our slain Messiah. Jesus is lifted up on that cross and all who choose to obey and look to Him, beg for forgiveness, and trust their human nature to His grace, shall be saved. The gift of salvation, bought on Resurrection Sunday, mirrors the healing that was wrought by Moses' statue. Salvation requires obedience just like the deliverance from the fiery serpents. Just as the victims of the serpents had to turn and look on the statue for healing, we must repent of our sins, look to Jesus' cross, and be baptized in His name according to Acts 2:38. The beautiful pattern of salvation in Numbers mirrors the salvation found in the Gospels.

You might have heard that comparison before. Jesus lifted up on His cross, drawing all men to Him, is comparable to that brazen serpent the ancient Hebrews depended upon for their healing. But do you know what happened to the brazen serpent 1,000 years after Moses' time? The Bible records in 2 Kings 18:1-4 that the brazen serpent was destroyed.

1 Now it came to pass in the third year of Hoshea son of Elah king of Israel, that Hezekiah the son of Ahaz king of Judah began to reign.

2 Twenty and five years old was he when he began to reign; and he reigned twenty and nine years in Jerusalem. His mother's name also was Abi, the daughter of Zachariah.

3 And he did that which was right in the sight of the Lord, according to all that David his father did.

4 He removed the high places, and brake the images, and cut down the groves, and brake in pieces the brasen serpent that Moses had made: for unto those days the children of Israel did burn incense to it: and he called it Nehushtan. (KJV)

When I first read that scripture, I was perplexed. I thought, "If this comparison points to Jesus on the cross, then why in the world was the brass serpent destroyed?" Like any teacher or preacher with a question, I delved into the Word to discover the answer.

If you are like me, the word that sticks out to you in this text is "Nehushtan." Easton's Bible Dictionary records that Nehushtan means:

> ***a name of contempt given to the serpent Moses had made in the wilderness (Numbers 21:8), and which Hezekiah destroyed because the children of Israel began to regard it as an idol and "burn incense to it." The lapse of nearly one thousand years had invested the "brazen serpent" with a mysterious sanctity; and in order to deliver the people from their infatuation, and impress them with the idea of its worthlessness, Hezekiah called it, in contempt, "Nehushtan," a brazen thing, a mere piece of brass***

Easton's summary evinces that the people forgot the Designer of the brazen serpent and began to worship the object itself.

I know this sermon must sound like an odd Easter message, so let me explain why I'm exploring this topic. We are living through a discouraging time right now, amen? I never thought that I would be living through a pandemic! If we are not careful, we will lose sight of what is important and place our trust in things or even spiritual gifts instead of simply trusting the Creator. What's more, if we are not careful, we will try to cling to an old experience that is no longer able to sustain us just as the Hebrews in our text from 2 Kings. After all, they were clinging to a wilderness experience when God wanted to give them something so much more miraculous. He wanted them to know Him in Spirit and in truth. Hezekiah, understanding God's desire, called the serpent Nehushtan, a derogatory name, because he was trying to rid Israel of idolatry. He wanted them to worship God.

How did this object become an idol? How did something that God created to bring healing devolve into Nehushtan? After all, Moses did as he was told. God Himself designed the idea of the brazen serpent. However, God does not want us to be satisfied with yesterday's experiences, especially if they were wilderness experiences. Furthermore, the people took what God had given them and began to worship it instead of worshipping Him. In essence, they were going through the motions. They were worshipping an idol without focusing on the meaning behind the statue.

When Jesus showed up in Samaria and talked to the woman at the well several hundred years later, He must have been sorely displeased to learn that not much had changed among His creation. In fact, in John chapter 4, He tells her, "You people of Samaria do not even know what it is that you worship. The time will come when God's followers will worship Him in Spirit and truth." Friends, I surely hope that time has arrived for us.

In our state of discouragement right now, I encourage us to seek God with more zeal than we have ever sought Him before. Like the ancient Hebrews, we are in desperate need of healing. If we can't cry out in Spirit and in truth during a global crisis such as the current Coronavirus pandemic, are we really worshipping Him at all? The salvation of Moses' day is not enough. The worship recorded in 2 Kings 18 is not enough. We need to understand the magnitude of our worship–its vast importance.

After all, salvation is revolutionary. It is not a brazen, wilderness experience. When Jesus conquered death, hell, and the grave, He revolutionized salvation. Our old experiences, old ways of thinking, and spiritual moments of yesteryear are not all that God has for us. Hezekiah's subjects were trying to worship God outside of obedience. They focused on the wrong thing instead of on the right God. They put God on stage and worshipped an object. They tried to design their own worship when God wanted their obedience. They tried to put God in a box.

Speaking of boxes, I want to consider the burial of Jesus in more detail. In Jewish tradition, the bodies were wrapped in linen shrouds and placed in family tombs. After a year or more passed, an ossuary, or bone box, was taken into the tomb after the flesh had decayed. The deceased's bones were placed in the box, inscribed with his or her name, and placed back in the caverns of the tomb. In this way, one tomb could hold many more bodies. Archaeologists have discovered ossuaries of famous people mentioned in the Bible; in the 1970s, in fact, the ossuary of James the brother of Jesus was discovered. Caiaphas's bone box has also been found.

Guess who doesn't have a bone box? Jesus was only in that tomb for three days! His flesh was glorified! There was no need for a visit a year later. There was absolutely no putting God in a box.

The problem with humanity is that we are still trying to put God in a box. That is why we are so discouraged right now. That is why some people have no idea how salvation works, and they have no faith that God can keep them through this current spiritual storm. Unfortunately, they are relying on a spiritual experience that they might have had as a child, some distant memory of how religion was supposed to work, and they have tried to put God in a box. They want to compartmentalize Him. They do not want to be obedient and look on Him or lift Him up in their lives. Instead, they want God to magically appear out of the box, do their bidding, and resign Himself back to the box like some mystical genie in a bottle. What mockery!

God is not to be mocked. He designed salvation as an ongoing process that requires our obedience and pursuit of greater understanding with each day that passes. Resurrection is power–power that is not hanging like the serpent or rattling in a limestone ossuary. His name is not a name relegated to an inscription on a bone box, but it is the name above all names! His creation must worship that name in spirit and in truth. It must be honored, revered, and spoken over our lives, for by His name, we are saved! (Acts 4:12).

Is He a way of life for you? Do you really look to Him for everything? Do you bring Him your discouragement, or do you murmur against Him and His leaders when things don't go your way?

In short, do you try to put Him in a box?

If you do not have resurrection power in your life during this age of political corruption and mass persuasion, you desperately need to change that! If you are not worshipping the Giver of Life instead of His gifts, I do not know how you are going to emerge victoriously while the enemy is raging. I don't know about you, but if I am going to have to face the enemy, I don't want to have to fool with getting my God out of a box to go to battle for me. I want instant access to resurrection power that guarantees I am going to be victorious.

Let me offer you this advice. Do not worship the gifts of the Spirit. Do not worship prophecy, tongues, healing (such as what the serpent represented), discernment, knowledge, wisdom, or interpretation. Instead, worship the one true God. Do not murmur against Him or His leaders and don't put Him in a box that you dust off once a week or even less than that. He is not on a pole, He is not on a cross, and He is not in a bone box. He is alive forevermore!

The significance of the number seven is quite pervasive throughout scripture. It denotes completion and perfection. There are seven churches, seven angels, seven trumpets, and seven seals in John's revelation. Jesus, before He cheated the ossuary, uttered the seven sayings chronicled in the gospels. In fact, one of those sayings was to His own mother who stood at the foot of the cross, looking up at her dying son. He uttered, "Woman, behold thy son" and then charged His dear disciple to take care of her.

Interestingly enough, seven bones form the human eye socket. The Hebrews had to engage those seven bones when they looked on the brazen serpent to receive their healing. That's right! In order to receive healing in a completely different part of the body, they had to start with the bones that house the eye. In order for Mary and Jesus' beloved disciple to receive His last instruction, they had to engage the seven bones of the eye to look upon Him even though the sight was brutal to behold.

God has decreed the importance of spiritual vision from the genesis of His creation. Each time that the Lord created light, beauty, or order out of the dark emptiness, Moses records in Genesis that "God **saw** that it was good." That phrase appears six times in the Creation story, and on the seventh day, God sanctified the goodness He had seen. Later, in Proverbs 29:18, the wise writer captures God's declaration that "Where there is no vision, my people perish." Finally, in Joel 2:28, the prophet looks toward a spiritual revival marked by young men who shall "see visions."

Fast forward a few centuries. When Saul of Tarsus persecutes the outpouring of the Holy Spirit prophesied by Joel, God strikes him with blindness! In order to change the course of the entire Christian church, Jesus starts just beyond the seven bones of the eye. Once He had Saul's eyes, He operated on his heart. Truly, our spiritual vision often dictates the course of our lives and the lives of every person we meet.

I have to stop here and ask you a question. What are you looking at? You might be hurting in an area of your spiritual body that seems far removed from your eyes, but according to the Word, our discernment, our vision, is the key to life. Without it, we perish. Refusing to look at that brazen serpent meant certain death for the ancient Hebrews. Refusing to look at the cross means certain death for us. Refusing to look toward Him in times of calamities, corruption, brutality, and even pandemics will certainly cause us to live a life far beneath the one He wants for us. Though it might be easy to fixate on our pain or heartbreak, we must learn to focus on Him.

If you suffer a fracture of the eye socket, you will experience double vision and severe pain. What happens in the physical realm is mirrored in the spiritual. Double vision, after all, leads Christians to sway with every wind of doctrine. In fact, James teaches us that a "double-minded man is unstable in all of his ways." I venture to guess that a double-minded man or woman invariably suffers from double vision as well.

Today's world requires stability. We need keen vision, clear minds, and unwavering faith–the kind of faith you get when the Lord strikes you blind on the road to Damascus and gives you a completely new way of seeing. If you are experiencing spiritual or emotional turmoil, I advise you to take note of what your eyes are fixed upon. Start at those seven bones.

REFLECTION:

1. What personal challenges are you facing right now?

2. Is your church or community experiencing struggles? Describe them.

3. What national or global challenges are frightening to you?

4. In what ways can you correct your spiritual vision to restore peace? Are there any scriptures from this chapter or previous chapters that might help? If so, list them. Keep the verses handy and in sight.

Chapter Eight

Believe When the Money Fails

It is written, That man shall not live by bread alone, but by every word of God-Luke 4:4 (KJV)

At the close of the last chapter, I asked you to consider what you were looking at. In the middle of a pandemic, I am sure many of us are tempted to focus on the problems of the day. We might be overwhelmed with worries regarding our finances, our health, our families, and our jobs. Many of us have never experienced such a frightening calamity in our lifetime. Stay at home orders, closed churches and synagogues, interruptions of supply and demand in our food distribution, and impossible-to-purchase items such as hand sanitizer or disinfectant spray are just a few tell-tale signs that we haven't fully emerged from this global crisis that touched down in the United States during January of 2020 and still lingers at the close of May.

"What are you looking at?" I asked. The truth is you might be looking at your circumstances and wondering where in the world God is.

I think we feel that kind of overwhelming doubt because many of us have never witnessed a pandemic before. We are not used to being primary sources. Simon Sinek, one of my favorite internet personalities and authors, pointed out that if people lived to be a thousand years-old, Covid-19 would not be so scary because we would have already experienced several pandemics by now. He also pointed out that the businesses that will survive this economic disaster are the businesses that will adapt. Indeed, disease and famine and pestilence and drought are all part of the human experience and have been for ages. God always has people who are ready to adapt, and as Sinek said, survive.

When our church in Manville reopened for regular service, Pastor Turner asked me to speak. I wasn't quite sure what to say to the congregation, but God reminded me that the Bible records many global calamities such as what we are experiencing. In fact, many have said, "I never thought this would happen in America." Do you know who else never thought that wide-scale disaster could happen to them even after warnings? The Egyptians.

Simon Sinek is right. If our lifetimes spanned centuries, we would have seen pandemics before. What we have to realize is that God has always been in control, and He still is. He was God in Egypt even though Egypt didn't know it, and He is God in America whether we realize it or not. We can't look to another Pharaoh. We have to look toward God.

When the ladies came to Jesus' tomb early on that third morning, they were worried about how they would be able to move the huge stone that covered the doorway. They were focused on a problem, so much so that they didn't realize that the power of God and His angelic force had already rolled the stone from the tomb's entrance. How many worried, fearful steps did they take before realizing that the problem had already been solved? With death all around them, I'm sure it was easy to fixate on the obstacles that they needed to overcome. However, God is never going to ask us to move something that we can't move. Instead of focusing on the obstacles, instead of focusing on the negative, let's fix our eyes on Jesus, for He always has a plan in times of calamity.

How do I know that? Let me just say that I am well acquainted with the story of Joseph, an anointed leader, who saw Egypt through a large-scale famine because he knew the One True God.

Let me share that story with you now, and I pray it will give you hope when you find yourself surrounded by more problems than you think you have solutions for. It certainly reminded me that even in a pandemic, God is still God.

It is an honor to address my brothers and sisters in Christ from behind this sacred desk. We have missed worshipping together and praying for one another. Now that we are back, let us never take for granted the right to assemble ourselves together as the Book of Hebrews instructs us to do. I'd like to begin my sharing Genesis 47: 13-20 (KJV) with you:

13 And there was no bread in all the land; for the famine was very sore, so that the land of Egypt and all the land of Canaan fainted by reason of the famine.

14 And Joseph gathered up all the money that was found in the land of Egypt, and in the land of Canaan, for the corn which they bought: and Joseph brought the money into Pharaoh's house.

15 And when money failed in the land of Egypt, and in the land of Canaan, all the Egyptians came unto Joseph, and said, Give us bread: for why should we die in thy presence? for the money faileth.

16 And Joseph said, Give your cattle; and I will give you for your cattle, if money fail.

17 And they brought their cattle unto Joseph: and Joseph gave them bread in exchange for horses, and for the flocks, and for the cattle of the herds, and for the asses: and he fed them with bread for all their cattle for that year.

18 When that year was ended, they came unto him the second year, and said unto him, We will not hide it from my lord, how that our money is spent; my lord also hath our herds of cattle; there is not ought left in the sight of my lord, but our bodies, and our lands:

19 Wherefore shall we die before thine eyes, both we and our land? buy us and our land for bread, and we and our land will be servants unto Pharaoh: and give us seed, that we may live, and not die, that the land be not desolate.

20 And Joseph bought all the land of Egypt for Pharaoh; for the Egyptians sold every man his field, because the famine prevailed over them: so the land became Pharaoh's.

They say that history has a way of repeating itself, and we know that Egypt in the Old Testament represents the world outside of God's will for they did not worship the One True God that Joseph knew as Lord. What draws my attention to this chapter on this day is the fact that I see our own country heading down the same path that these Egyptians were following. I would like us to focus on verse 15 for a moment.

And when money failed in the land of Egypt, and in the land of Canaan, all the Egyptians came unto Joseph, and said, Give us bread: for why should we die in thy presence? for the money faileth.

Is it any surprise that the Egyptians cried out to the only godly man in the nation? Even Pharaoh himself recognized that Joseph was a man set apart, and he handed the keys to the kingdom to the Hebrew. He trusted Joseph enough to make him second in command over the entire nation.

It is important for us to realize that Joseph is a type and shadow of the Savior to come; indeed, he saved the people from famine and economic collapse in this chapter of Genesis. He brought the world safely through the perilous times that it had found itself in. The people went to him and essentially cried, "Why should we die when you know how to save us? Give us bread for the money faileth." That subject is what I'd like to address in the next few moments. We must believe when the money fails.

I'd like for you to notice how the Egyptians, the people who didn't know God, reacted in these desperate times. First, they sought someone who had an anointing to deal with the catastrophe. There came a day according to verse 15 when the money indeed failed in the land and they began looking for someone to help them find bread. Now, to get a picture of this you have to understand what a vast and powerful empire Egypt was during Joseph's life. It was rich beyond measure. It boasted a long line of kings. It was far advanced in comparison to the surrounding areas, and the people had put their trust in gods that they (with the help of their money) could build. They didn't serve a God who could build them up; rather, they served gods that they had to build. Thus, their approaching Joseph was surprising. For them to come to him and say, "We realize our money is not going to do us any good; it has lost all value, the economy is decimated and all we want is bread," was astonishing! For them to come to Joseph acknowledging the complete failure of their monetary system was truly unthinkable. Before the seven years of famine set in, no one except for Joseph, the Interpreter of Dreams, would have ever thought that this world economy would fail. The Egyptians never fathomed that they would find themselves begging before this young man who had risen from the dungeon to the palace. Yet, here they are in Genesis doing just that.

Joseph instructs them first to sell their livestock: livestock they could no longer take care of; livestock that would have starved to death in their care because of the dearth in the land; horses and flocks that would have been no use to them starving in the fields. Without modern refrigeration, they could not save the meat, so they needed the grain. Joseph benevolently gave them bread for their livestock when the money failed within a year's time. Sometimes, salvation requires that we let go of the things we think we need and cling to what can sustain us when all else fails.

Remember, Joseph foreshadows our Savior. The people have come to him and have given him what they possessed but could not care for. If we think for one moment that God does not already own everything, then we have fooled ourselves. He created all things, and all things belong to Him. In the end, when all of our crises wind down, the world is going to stand in discovery just like the Egyptians and say, "We have nothing left, and the Lord...He has it all!"

Despite Joseph's benevolence, the famine rages on. The Egyptians once again come to Joseph and declare, "We have nothing left except ourselves, our bodies, and our land." Would you believe they actually propositioned Joseph to buy them as slaves? In verse 19, they make the deal. They willingly sold themselves into bondage and gave up all that they owned! Why? Because the money failed, they became servants to Pharaoh. All for bread!

Let's stop and consider the state of affairs in our world today. Our economy, too, is crumbling, but the spiritual famine and moral decline we see all around us is far more important than that. People have sold themselves into bondage to all manner of sin; and just like Egypt, fair nations have become a metropolis of sin and desolation. The world's people chase after all manner of unrighteousness, thinking nothing of it because they have put their trust in everything else but God. They trust systems that will fail.

The world is being the world, and the Church is just going to have to step up and be the Church. We have to be the voice of Joseph to a starving Egypt. Joseph moved the people to the city so that he could distribute the needed bread more easily and efficiently. The world is coming, Church. They will come to the places that are ready to distribute the bread of life. We had better take a lesson from Joseph and prepare for them. Isaiah declared, "Enlarge your tents!" The Church had better heed Isaiah's ancient words.

How? By declaring that God turned the picture of Genesis 47 on its head! The people came and they sold themselves into bondage for bread. However, if you will consider John 6:32-35, you will see that God's son, born in Bethlehem (which literally means "House of Bread"), ransomed the people rather than enslaving them:

32 Then Jesus said unto them, Verily, verily, I say unto you, Moses gave you not that bread from heaven; but my Father giveth you the true bread from heaven.

33 For the bread of God is he which cometh down from heaven, and giveth life unto the world.

34 Then said they unto him, Lord, evermore give us this bread.

35 And Jesus said unto them, I am the bread of life: he that cometh to me shall never hunger; and he that believeth on me shall never thirst.

Clearly, Jesus flipped the whole situation that we found in Genesis. Instead of the people selling themselves into bondage for bread, the Bread actually redeemed the people out of their bondage. We–the Elect, the Bride, the Church–we have this truth. We know this deliveranc. The world is going to show up and say, "Church, the money fails!" or "Preacher, the doctor fails!" or "Pastor, my choices fail!" or "Minister, the world's way fails!" When they do, we are going to have to lead like Joseph. We are going to have to say, "It is OK. What you really need is the Bread. We know where the Bread is. We know how to get it. We know that it is the only thing that will pull you out of the bondage you have found yourself in–bondage to a system that faileth."

If you are miserable, my friend, you are in bondage. If you are unhappy, you don't have to stay in Egypt. Instead of selling yourself for bread, let the Bread pull you out of captivity. He is the answer to every trouble. Take "money" out of this sermon's title, and substitute any word you want–the message remains the same. The law fails. The court fails. Jobs fail. Leaders fail. Medicine fails. Whatever has failed you, please realize that God is above it. The answer to your turmoil is John 6:35.

Church, be ready when they say, "Evermore give us this bread!" Lead them to the storehouse!

Many say that desperate times call for desperate measures. However, I'd like to suggest that desperate times call for faith and hope. Joseph, the hero of the Genesis account we just read, believed that faith and hope start at the bone. In fact, his dying wish was a prophecy concerning Israel's exodus from bondage in Egypt. His story closes in Genesis 50: 22-26 (KJV):

22 And Joseph dwelt in Egypt, he, and his father's house: and Joseph lived an hundred and ten years.

23 And Joseph saw Ephraim's children of the third generation: the children also of Machir the son of Manasseh were brought up upon Joseph's knees.

24 And Joseph said unto his brethren, I die: and God will surely visit you, and bring you out of this land unto the land which he sware to Abraham, to Isaac, and to Jacob.

25 And Joseph took an oath of the children of Israel, saying, God will surely visit you, and ye shall carry up my bones from hence.

26 So Joseph died, being an hundred and ten years old: and they embalmed him, and he was put in a coffin in Egypt.

Joseph is not just making a final request. He is prophesying that God will once again restore His people and lead them to a promised land. "God will surely visit you," he tells them. It was not a request; it was an order because it was a prophecy. He told them that they "SHALL" carry his bones from Egypt, a land of false idols and corruption. It was an ordinance, a decree pointing toward their eventual departure from the land that claimed him as a slave all those years earlier when his brothers betrayed him.

Centuries passed and the leaders of Egypt eventually forgot Joseph's greatness, but his prophecy remained. When Moses arrived on the scene, Egyptian taskmasters, cruel and bitter, had enslaved the Hebrews. Years later, when Moses led his people out of slavery, Exodus 13:19 records that he "took the bones of Joseph with him."

Isn't it interesting that Moses refers to the carrying of "bones," when Joseph was clearly embalmed according to Genesis 50? In reality, his embalmed body was carried out of Egypt, the place where his brothers sold him into slavery, slavery that he eventually surmounted. Let's not miss the symbolism here. According to Jewish writer Ora Horn Prouser: "Moses should be speaking about carrying [Joseph's] body, but the emphasis is on bones. Embalming is particularly Egyptian. Ignoring the embalming is part of leaving Egypt behind as the people set out to their particularly Israelite future." Joseph was a visionary, and he believed all that God showed him. His faith led to his eventual mentioning in the Hebrews Hall of Fame! In fact, Hebrews 11:22 records that "By faith Joseph, when he died, made mention of the departing of the children of Israel; and gave commandment concerning his bones" (KJV). Burial was particularly important in Jewish culture, and "Joseph was willing to base his future resting place on his belief that his people would leave Egypt" (Prouser). Now that's faith!

Of course, I'm not telling you to be concerned about your literal resting place. I'm saying that your future depends on your coming out of slavery to sin, shame, and sorrow. You do that by starting at the bone-the place where you were betrayed and fell into bondage far from the promises and prophecies that the Lord has spoken over your life. Be like Joseph: Refuse to stay in a place God did not create for you, serving systems that will eventually fail. In order to rise above the political chaos, the economic uncertainty, and the social injustices we are witnessing in this dark hour, we must (like Joseph) start at the bone!

REFLECTION:

1. Describe a personal betrayal you have endured. In what ways did this betrayal "enslave" you?

2. How did God move (or how is He currently moving) to release you from that pain?

3. What else needs to happen in order for you to feel healed from this betrayal?

4. What active steps can you take in that healing process?

5. How might Joseph's story help you?

Chapter Nine

Battle in the Pit!

Be sober-minded; be watchful. Your adversary the devil prowls around like a roaring lion, seeking someone to devour-1 Peter 5:8 (ESV)

Before I ever preached the sermon about the collapse of Egypt's monetary system, I took the pulpit in January of 2020 having no idea of the storms that were brewing in our country. Even though Covid-19 had likely been an active contagion months prior, many of us entered 2020 with high expectations for a blessed year. We did not anticipate the complete shutting down of our economy, our churches, our schools, our lives. "We'll have plenty in 2020" was the resounding mantra that many Americans proclaimed. By March, the world as we knew it had drastically changed. Covid-19 and the ensuing effort to "flatten the curve" of exposure and infection so that our health care system wouldn't collapse under the weight of this disease hit in the winter months–the time of snow–and strangled us by spring!

As I revisited the first sermon that I preached in January 2020, I was awed at how God's word is always ahead of calamity. Before we begin blaming God for the turmoil we are experiencing, I would like to remind us that sickness and disease are part of the human condition brought on by original sin and the work of the enemy. God does not propagate death and disease; that is Satan's realm. He started with the lie to Eve when he whispered, "You won't die," knowing that her disobedience would start the chain reaction from luxurious life in Eden to death in darkness outside the garden. Clearly, disease entered the picture when Satan entered the garden and turned it into a graveyard of lost privileges and possibilities. But as Elevation Worship's song declares, God turns "graves into gardens." Only God's love, only His sacrificial Son, can bring us back to life!

No matter where it started, the fact remains that disease is here. Isn't it strange how there are "seasons" of flu and other viruses? We have seasonal flu, seasonal colds, seasonal allergies, and a whole host of viruses that seem to thrive during certain periods of time. In particular, influenza and other flu-like illnesses seem to love the cold weather: They are most active in the time of snow. Satan works the same way. He launches offensive spiritual strikes against us when we are least able to counter with a defensive effort. That is why the next sermon that I am going to share with you is so important. It illustrates how we can take the offensive and stop him in his tracks!

In Chapter 8, I discussed how God placed Joseph in a position of authority that would allow his people to survive the famine that threatened to cripple the most impressive kingdom of that day. Long before Joseph became Zaphnath-Paaneah, second in command of the Egyptian empire, his brothers threw him in a pit and sold him into slavery. His battle to survive and realize the dreams that God shared with him in Genesis 36 actually began in that pit. The question we have to ask ourselves is how we will react in the pits of our lives.

If that question weighs heavily on your heart right now, I'd like to introduce you to a man named Benaiah, a man who knew how to battle in a pit during the winter season. Join me at the little church in Manville for the sermon, "In the Time of Snow."

I am often amazed when I read the Bible and discover riveting stories of fascinating people who are briefly mentioned in a few verses. They often mark a tiny spot on the pages of history and then vanish from the rest of the holy record. Their influence is remarkable, and often their feats are miraculous despite the fact that their entire lives are summarized in two or three verses. Men such as Shamgar with his ox-goad, Jabez with his brief prayer, and Benaiah in his cold pit come to mind. In fact, Benaiah is the hero I'd like to consider now. The son of Jehoiada (as Benaiah is called) is mentioned only a handful of times in the Bible, and we must be careful not to confuse him with other men of the same name. When the ancient writers mention the son of Jehoiada, you can bet that he is performing an amazing feat for David's–and later Solomon's–kingdom. Three verses in the Old Testament commemorate two of his amazing deeds. Let's read 2 Samuel 23: 20-22 (KJV):

20 And Benaiah the son of Jehoiada, the son of a valiant man, of Kabzeel, who had done many acts, he slew two lion-like men of Moab: he went down also and slew a lion in the midst of a pit in time of snow:

21 And he slew an Egyptian, a goodly man: and the Egyptian had a spear in his hand; but he went down to him with a staff, and plucked the spear out

of the Egyptian's hand, and slew him with his own spear.

22 These things did Benaiah the son of Jehoiada, and had the name among three mighty men.

In the book of 2 Samuel, we are given an account of David's mighty men. If you don't know anything about this ragtag bunch of men, let me fill you in. They were courageous and bold, they were strong and mighty, they were feared by many. You see, they didn't have the best reputation in the world. They were known as scoundrels, they had seen some tough times, and they had lived less than godly lives. Like many of us, they had made some disastrous mistakes. They were not what you would call righteous. They were not what you would call godly. Yet, God in His infinite wisdom chose these men to surround and protect His anointed king. God saw purpose in them even though many people in that day would have discounted, disliked, or denounced them.

What I find fascinating about Benaiah is that he made the choice to go down into a pit, into a circumstance, to kill a lion that he had pursued. The ground was slippery and icy for it was the time of snow: a time during which many of us would have hunkered down in our warm beds, trying to get through the winter day. Conversely, here is a man who actually chooses to go down into a pit to kill a predator. I don't know about you, but if I had been in a predator/prey relationship and the lion had fled into a pit to escape, I would have been more than happy to let him stay in there alone. I would have been praising God that I had escaped, and I would have left that lion in the pit by itself. That decision, however, would have been a poor one. How many of you know that sometimes you have to slay your demons or they will live to rise up another day? Had he let that lion live, he very well may have faced this powerful beast again.

Some scholars surmise that the lion had sustained an injury and perhaps had crept into the pit to recover. They suggest that Benaiah's slaying of the lion was actually a mercy killing (Cole-Rous). Nevertheless, the fact remains that Benaiah chose to enter the pit on a snowy day when he could have returned home. I think his choice regarding the pit is why I find this story so compelling.

Let me explain. The Bible gives all sorts of accounts of pits. There are pits that our enemies devise for us, there are pits that we fall into ourselves, and there are pits that our enemy will try to lure us into. In order for us to live a victorious life, we are going to have to understand some things about pits–the enemy's territory.

We encounter a famous pit in the Book of Genesis when Joseph's brothers, overcome with jealousy, devise the plan to throw him into the pit and then sell him to the first slave trader that comes along. Of all the pits in our lives, I think this type is the most hurtful because members of our family or church family should be the last people to rise up against us. After all, Joseph was just sharing what God had given to him. He could have used a little more wisdom in that sharing, but he was excited about what God was doing in his life. Have you ever been there? Have you ever felt excited about how God is blessing you? Have you ever found yourself in a situation trying to do your very best for God only to find that those who call themselves Christians and should love you the most are devising plans to destroy you? Yes, when your own brothers rise up against you, the betrayal wounds, scars, and leaves you sorrowful.

Imagine Josephs' feelings of rejection and betrayal as they cast him into that pit and then sold him as a slave. Imagine how he later felt in the prison after Potiphar's wife falsely accused him and it seemed God had abandoned him. Still, Joseph found purpose in the pit just as he did in the palace. Joseph's secret to success was his controlled reactions. Wherever God placed him, he purposed in his heart to do the very best for God that he could do. Of course, God knew all the while that He was going to use Joseph to bring reconciliation to Jacob's family.

Yes! There is a day coming, Friend, in the lives of all Christian believers when they will realize the essence of Romans 8:28–everything working toward their good! It only follows the time of snow, the time of pits and prisons. It is a day of reconciliation. Of restoration. Joseph's early circumstances would eventually change, and his dreams and visions would eventually come to pass. Maybe you are living in a season of pits and prisons right now, but do not lose sight of the fact that God sees the bigger picture. Find out what you can do to serve God where you are, and throw yourself into it until you hear the call out of the pit.

As we journey through God's Holy Word, we discover other types of pits that we construct through our own actions. Not every pit in your life is devised by your enemies.

In the book of Judges, for example, we read about a coward turned judge. Gideon was hiding out in the winepress, a makeshift pit if you will, because he was afraid of the Midianites. You see, the Midianites were enemies of God's people; each time God's people produced something good, the enemy would show up to take it. Because of Gideon's fear, he finds himself down in the winepress, the pit, hoping to keep his goods safe from the enemy. Can you relate to Gideon? Every time you try to produce something good in your life, the enemy shows up and steals it from you? Because of this constant abuse, you might have become fearful, and you possibly have retreated into a pit of your own making. This was Gideon's truth. He was so defeated that when God showed up to call him to a special task, Gideon's self-esteem was so low that he kept testing God. God literally had to coax him out of that pit! Had he stayed in the winepress, had he continued to hide, he never would have defeated the Midianites. At the beginning of his story, though, the biggest difference between Benaiah and Gideon was their interaction with the pit. Benaiah relentlessly pursued all that troubled him into the pit while Gideon cowered in it. His story illustrates that God can embolden us no matter what pit we have found ourselves in.

Finally, we have to consider King David. He declares in Psalms 40:1-3 (KJV):

1 I waited patiently for the Lord; and he inclined unto me, and heard my cry.

2 He brought me up also out of an horrible pit, out of the miry clay, and set my feet upon a rock, and established my goings.

3 And he hath put a new song in my mouth, even praise unto our God: many shall see it, and fear, and shall trust in the Lord.

Even kings find themselves in horrible pits. This Psalm comforts me in that verse 3 points out how God can turn our pits into praise reports! Pits transform us into victors who testify of God's powerful love to the point that others will "see it, and fear, and shall trust in the Lord."

I've talked to you about a dream interpreter, a judge, and a king–all of whom found their way into a pit. Why then is our society so condemning of people who have experienced pitfalls? If God's chosen king ended up in a pit, what makes us think that we aren't going to experience times of snow and pitfalls as well? Truthfully, I think we are terribly harsh toward people in pits. We don't know what dreams they might be interpreting there. We don't know what callings are being placed on their lives in the winepress. We don't know what kingdoms God is going to entrust them with. The church's job is to help them find their way out of trouble and to assist them in reaching their full potential in the kingdom of God. Really, when you think about it in that sense, the church itself should become a pit.

Let me tell you what I mean. Let's consider 2 Samuel 23: 20-22 again. Here we see Benaiah who had been put to the test. Notice that before he ever killed the lion, he slew two men that were compared to lions. The men are called "lion-like men of Moab." Can you relate to Benaiah? Perhaps you too have faced a terrible battle. At the time, it certainly was the worst thing you could have imagined, but then suddenly, you were thrown into a new battle, even worse than the preceding one. You might be in such a battle now. Perhaps you have realized that the first enemy was indeed daunting, but this new struggle? It **IS** the real deal! Notice that Benaiah didn't run from the real battle. He chased that lion into a pit, cornered him, and slew him. How was he able to do that? He had been prepared before he ever chased that lion. He had fought two foes that were like it and was then able to take on the real thing. In fact, Benaiah's name means, "to build." In the same way that he protected and bolstered the kingdom, God protected and built him up for bigger and loftier feats. God is doing the same with us. Step by step, battle by battle, pit by pit, He is conforming us to His image so that we can accomplish our purpose in the kingdom.

Let me ask you some questions today.

What has left you cold?

What has been slippery to navigate?

What has been treacherous to battle?

What is **YOUR** time of snow?

What battles have left you so tired that now that you're facing the ultimate test, you aren't sure how to win? You know what you need? You need a pit! Benaiah needed a place to corner that beast, and so do you! Friend, an altar of prayer is where you can corner that lion! And the snow? Never fret! All of those obstacles you are facing will ultimately help you track the enemy down just as tracks in the snow eventually lead the hunter to the prize!

Let the church be your pit in time of snow! That is why the church exists. Let prayer be your weapon, sharpened and keen enough to take on the beasts that prowl, seeking whom they may devour. Benaiah took the defensive. He tracked the lion, cornered him and defeated him once and for all. It is time for God's people to stand up and be proactive rather than reactive!

Let me explain something about a church that is full of love. It does not judge people who have been in the pit because we have all spent time there. Whether our brothers or sisters dug it for us, whether our enemies forced us into it, or whether our own sin, like King David's, cast us down into the trap. If you have found yourself in Benaiah's shoes, do not wait until conditions are better to take this enemy down. Track him in time of snow, a time he thinks not, and corner him at the altar of prayer!

Before the young shepherd boy ascended to his throne, King David, like Benaiah, emerged victorious from a battle with fearsome beasts. He recounts the story to King Saul in 1 Samuel 17. In verses 34-35, he declares that "When a lion or a bear came and took a lamb from the flock, [David] went out after him and attacked him, and rescued *it* from his mouth" and finally "seized *him* by his beard and struck him and killed him" (NASB). While David might have had a shepherd's staff or other weapon, it is interesting to note that he used his bare hands to grab the animal by its hair. David knew how to use what he had at his disposal when tasked with the responsibility of saving his father's lambs.

While two hands might not sound like much, David was actually using 54 bones (since 27 bones make up the human hand) to secure victory. We know by now that we have to start at the bone, and David certainly did that. Just as Benaiah was trained to be a hero, David started as a shepherd whose encounters with the lion and bear prepared him to stand up to Goliath and later to lead a group of valiant warriors. When God sees that we will faithfully use what He has given us to complete the tasks He assigns to us, we will eventually graduate to bigger and better weapons. After all, David later used a slingshot and finally a sword to sever

Goliath's head. However, we must not forget that he started with two strong hands! Don't be afraid to start at the bone.

Jesus did the same thing, you know. His father's lambs were threatened. We had strayed from the fold and needed reconciliation. While Peter envisioned a kingdom built on the sword, Jesus made him put that weapon away. Instead, like David seizing the lion, Jesus stretched His arms wide and allowed His hands to battle for us. He started at the bone, but those bones would soon be glorified. Like Samson on his way to his wedding feast, ripping the jaws of a lion apart, Christ fought for His Bride with nail-scarred hands that gripped the jaws of death and split the grave in two!

REFLECTION:

1. Trace your spiritual growth through a difficult battle in your past. How did the battle change you?

2. Describe a current battle that you are fighting. What active steps do you need to take to secure victory?

3. Do you tend to be reactive or proactive (like Benaiah)? What active steps do you need to take to be more proactive?

Chapter Ten

Be Righteous

When the righteous cry for help, the LORD hears and delivers them out of all their troubles-Psalm 34:17 (ESV)

This book began as a thought in November and evolved into a response to a command in December. Even though I had just published my first book in June of 2019, I felt the Lord instructing me to write this book in December of the same year. I planned to begin seriously drafting during summer when my job as a schoolteacher would halt for a few weeks. However, I am penning this last chapter on June 18; I am nearly finished with the book because I spent weeks, along with the rest of the country, sheltering at home. Clearly, I had time to write.

I hesitate to share what I felt the Lord saying to me in December because I know it will sound fabricated. However, my church family and my parents can attest to the truthfulness of my recollection because I shared it with Manville's congregation from the pulpit before we ever rang in the New Year. I'm sure we all hear God in different ways, and I don't know how to explain it other than a spiritual leading, but I distinctly remember God's three imperatives to me: Believe in the mission at Manville. Believe in healing. Write *Start at the Bone*. At the time, I did not even have the subtitle to the book. That would come to me on December 12, 2019. (Thanks to Google's version history, I can easily look that up). On that afternoon, God gave me the subtitle: *Healing for Our Churches and Ourselves*. When I think of how much the world has changed since December 12, 2019, I'm shaken.

I had absolutely no idea that a pandemic was approaching and that churches would shut down. I had no idea that sickness was about to descend upon our nation and that I would definitely need to have faith in healing. I had no idea that our country would be torn apart once again by racism and rioting. I did not understand in December 2019 that spiritual healing and renewal would be just as important as physical healing in the wake of Covid-19 and African American deaths resulting from excessive force by police officers. The heartbreaking story of Breonna Taylor, a 26 year-old EMT, who was fatally and egregiously shot by police officers during a "no knock" raid outraged the country in March. Just two months later, video footage from Minneapolis showed Derek Chauvin detaining George Floyd with a controversial neck hold. Floyd's subsequent death sent America to the brink as peaceful protests gave way to rioting and looting. I had no idea that we were heading to that precipice in 2020. I simply felt compelled to believe in healing long before I knew how much faith that would actually take.

Pastor Turner asked me to speak the Sunday following the burning of several U.S. cities. What could I say to a congregation following such a tragic week? I sought the Lord in prayer, and Isaiah chapter 3 unfolded for me. God plainly instructed me to tell the church and now my readers this: "Say to the righteous that it will go well with them for they will eat the fruit of their actions" (Isaiah 3:10, NASB).

If you have been the victim of prejudice and racism, I want you to believe in healing, too. As a white woman, I cannot speak to the black experience, but my first book speaks of the gender discrimination I have endured. Violence against women is still pervasive in this country, and disrespectful female stereotypes are still ubiquitous. I know what it is like to be disregarded, verbally and physically attacked, and constantly marginalized based on a human attribute that I could not choose. I discuss domestic violence and wide-sweeping marginalization at length in *The Trouble with Sticks*.

As I write these words, an amusing (I won't say funny) story comes to mind. Several years ago, in the 1990s, I was participating in an online Bible discussion. Everything was anonymous. I had a username that in no way identified who I actually was. It was CMACPD. I knew what the acronym meant, of course, but no one else did. Everyone on that discussion board just assumed I was male simply because I could discuss biblical exposition articulately and intelligently. When discussions of women's roles in the Bible eventually emerged, I began to sign my posts, "In Love, SIS CM." When I revealed my gender, the participants were shocked, but none of them could really explain why they naturally jumped to the erroneous conclusion that I was a man instead of a woman. They were not trying to be hurtful, but their assumptions testify to micro aggressive behavior toward women and minorities in this country. Simply put, God made me a white female. I had absolutely no say in the matter, and yet, somehow the female aspect of His creation angers some and bewilders many.

I have no idea how anyone can hate any aspects of God's creation. If you are a black woman, God made you female and black, and you are to be celebrated. If you are a black man, God made you male and black, and you are to be celebrated. If you are a white woman, God made you female and white, and you are to be celebrated. If you are a white man, God made you male and white, and you are to be celebrated. If you are brown, red, or yellow, you are to be celebrated. No matter your color. No matter your gender. You deserve respect as a creation of God, and my heart breaks for any man or woman of any color who has endured racism and oppression. How we can hate others based on God's design–a design we had no say in–completely baffles me!

You know what we can control? Look back to Isaiah 3:10. God instructs the prophet to "Say to the righteous." Righteousness, unlike color or gender, is a choice. We can choose to live righteously or not. In these turbulent times, my advice to all of us is to pursue righteousness, for our world closely resembles Isaiah's world in chapter 3 of his book. Join me in Manville one more time as I preach, "Beauty instead of Burning."

My sweet church family, I struggled and struggled to understand what the Lord wanted me to say to this congregation today after a week of injustice and brutality on the one hand, and rioting and looting on the other. This morning, God finally brought today's message into clarity for me.

The Lord says in Isaiah 3:10 "Say to the righteous that it will go well with them, for they will eat the fruit of their actions" (NASB). I am saying these words to you this afternoon. Stay righteous. Stay on the side of God. Do not turn to the left; do not turn to the right. God is promising that He is going to keep you through this perilous year!

Furthermore, recognize that righteous living does not discriminate. Whether you are white, black, brown, or any other color, righteousness moves God, and not our own because the scripture teaches that it is filthy in His sight. The Lord's grace and His name spoken over your life intercedes for you. If you are a believer of Christ, born again, baptized into the family name, then you are my brother and sister no matter your race, no matter your gender, no matter your color. Galatians 3:28 teaches us that **in Christ** there is neither male nor female, Greek nor Jew, bond nor free. Here in Paul's letter to the Galatian church is the answer to the calamity in our world today: We must get in Christ!

Let's consider the state of affairs in Judah during Isaiah's time. In Isaiah 3 we read:

5 And the people shall be oppressed, every one by another, and every one by his neighbour: the child shall behave himself proudly against the ancient, and the base against the honourable. (KJV)

We do not have to look very far to see oppression in this country. We do not have to look very far to see neighbors rising up against neighbors or young people lashing out at older people in anger. Clearly, our world closely resembles Isaiah's world. Isaiah goes on to describe Judah–and more specifically Zion–as a woman who strives to be beautiful; however, the Lord declares that He will destroy all of the ornaments and cosmetics that she uses to adorn herself. Consider verse 24:

24 And it shall come to pass, that instead of sweet smell there shall be stink; and instead of a girdle a rent; and instead of well set hair baldness; and instead of a stomacher a girding of sackcloth; and burning instead of beauty. (KJV)

That last phrase actually means that her skin will not be beautiful; it will be sunburnt instead. Since she is a metaphor for Judah, however, we can interpret the comparison to imply the destruction of the city. Judah was destined to experience burning instead of beauty.

As Minneapolis continues to burn, I'd like to offer this congregation hope today. I'd like to tell you that we can have beauty instead of burning. How? By pursuing righteousness. Remember that God told Isaiah to "Say to the righteous, that it shall be well with them: for they shall eat the fruit of their actions." God declares, "Tell the righteous people that everything will be well for them. They will enjoy the rich reward they have earned!"

How do we become righteous? This question echoes the question of the expert lawyer who asked Jesus what he could do to ensure his eternal reward. Jesus told him that he needed to love the Lord and his neighbors. The young man asked a follow-up question that no doubt revealed his true nature. He said, "Who is my neighbor?" In response, Jesus tells the narrative of the Good Samaritan to explain to the lawyer the true meaning of righteousness. His parable remains one of the most powerful treatises against racism that has ever been uttered. You see, the Jews hated the Samaritans. They often avoided travel through Samaria and would even go miles out of their way to avoid the city. They considered the Samaritans a "mixed race," and discounted them as inferior. Imagine the lawyer's confusion when Jesus told him this story recorded in Luke 10:30-37 (NIV):

30 In reply Jesus said: "A man was going down from Jerusalem to Jericho, when he was attacked by robbers. They stripped him of his clothes, beat him and went away, leaving him half dead.

31 A priest happened to be going down the same road, and when he saw the man, he passed by on the other side.

32 So too, a Levite, when he came to the place and saw him, passed by on the other side.

33 But a Samaritan, as he traveled, came where the man was; and when he saw him, he took pity on him.

34 He went to him and bandaged his wounds, pouring on oil and wine. Then he put the man on his own donkey, brought him to an inn and took care of him.

35 The next day he took out two denarii and gave them to the innkeeper. 'Look after him,' he said, 'and when I return, I will reimburse you for any extra expense you may have.'

36 "Which of these three do you think was a neighbor to the man who fell into the hands of robbers?"

37 The expert in the law replied, "The one who had mercy on him." Jesus told him, "Go and do likewise."

Because of his prejudicial biases, the lawyer never expected the Samaritan to be the hero of the story. However, when Jesus finished his account, the man had to admit that mercy and righteousness go hand in hand. Who is our neighbor? Whom should we love? Everyone! Even the ones you have been taught to hate. If we could show mercy instead of brutality, if we could pour in soothing oil instead of throwing firebrands in buildings, if we could help pay the bill for hurt and wrongdoing by being loving and compassionate, perhaps we could have beauty instead of burning.

As God's children, we are not supposed to be oppressive. As God's children, we are not supposed to be lawless and unrighteous, either. We are burning because of our failures, but God said it does not have to be this way. If we remain righteous, if we get in Christ, then the sins of our fathers will have no bearing on our lives. None of us is responsible for the actions of our ancestors, but we are responsible for our behavior now. We must strive to empathize with people who have been abused on Jericho's road. We do not have to accept responsibility for their pain, but we do need to acknowledge it. We also must do all that we can to model the behavior of the Good Samaritan.

In the words of Bob Goff, we must love "Everybody. Always." We must love each other, and the best way to love people is to point them to Christ. Again, how do we get in Christ? As my brother often preaches, we get in Christ through baptism into His name and Christ gets in us through the infilling of the Holy Spirit (Acts 2:38). I believe this country could take a gigantic leap–out of pandemics, out of racism, out of lawlessness–if those who are not in Christ would make the life-changing decision to accept the God of love and live righteously. As cities burn and innocents are murdered and hatred is spewed by this group and that, God says, "You don't have to be a part of that narrative. You can be righteous and I will reward you. I will give you beauty instead of ashes, beauty instead of burning."

Knowing what God instructed the prophet to say to the people, and knowing how much we need the Lord in the year 2020 and the ones to follow, how could we refuse to be righteous?

Get in Christ.

Stay in Christ.

Receive your reward!

REFLECTION:

1. In what ways are you like the Good Samaritan?

2. In what ways are you unlike the Good Samaritan?

3. What does righteousness mean to you?

4. What active steps can you take toward righteousness?

As I mentioned before, this book was the answer to a command that the Lord gave me in December before the ominous year of 2020 darkened the land. If you will notice, each chapter's title is given in the imperative–as a command, an action–that I'm asking you to consider.

I've asked you to overcome, lift, ride, and listen. I've asked you to look up and to lift your voice. I've told you to believe and battle and to be available and righteous. I'm quite demanding, it would seem. But I wouldn't ask these things of you if I didn't truly believe they would help you. After all, the work of a minister is to help. The most important advice I can give you is to start at the bone: your humanity. Remember, you are made in God's image, but you aren't yet conformed to that image. That process comes through sanctification, and all of the action verbs I have given you will help you in that process.

Let me take just a moment to finish at the bone as well. I have one last story to share with you. It comes from 2 Kings 13: 20-21 (NIV):

20 Elisha died and was buried. Now Moabite raiders used to enter the country every spring.
21 Once while some Israelites were burying a man, suddenly they saw a band of raiders; so they threw the man's body into Elisha's tomb. When the body

touched Elisha's bones, the man came to life and stood up on his feet.

I want you to notice that in verse 20, we learn that the raiders showed up every spring. They came when it was convenient, with the winter weather behind them, and began plundering. EVERY spring! You would think the Israelites would have prepared for the Moabites' attack. The word "suddenly" indicates that they were caught off guard.

I think America has been caught off guard as well. No one would have said in the summer of 2019 that a pandemic was about to erupt. However, discontent in this nation has been brewing for a long time, and we need to work together now to find solutions so that all Americans can enjoy life, liberty, and the pursuit of happiness in a safe, protected environment.

Friends, enemies are always going to show up. The Moabites showed up like clockwork every year! What makes us think that modern times are any different? Our country, our communities, our churches cannot bury their heads in the sand and pretend that hard times are not going to reappear. We will have other seasons of sickness. We will have other election years. We will have injustice and drought and famine and disease until the Lord takes us home. Thankfully, though, God's people and God's churches are not powerless!

Elisha was dead, but the spirit of God was alive in his bones. He still had power to bring that dead man back to life. That same spirit is what will raise you from the dead! Might I suggest that even though the church was quiet for a few weeks, and even though this country is reeling on a precipice, Christians still have enough power in their bones to unify our nation and breathe life into cities and communities that desperately need it?

Will we be ready when the dead and the dying walk through our church doors? Will we be a tomb turned pit where lion slayers can be born? Will we have power in our bones to bring about lasting change in the lives of people who are searching for an answer?

Will we start at the bone?

REFLECTION:

1. What are your biggest takeaways from this book?

2. What scriptures from this book particularly stood out to you? Why?

3. Examine the cover of the book. How does it convey the meaning of the book's central analogy (the comparison of the Christian and/or the Christian Church to the human skeleton)?

Works Cited

Boba. "What the Fetal Position Does for Your Baby." *Boba*, boba.com/blogs/news/what-the-fetal-position-does-for-your-baby-1.

"Bone Conduction: How It Works." Goldendance.co.jp, 22 Mar. 2019, www.goldendance.co.jp/English/boneconduct/01.html.

"Ear Bone." *Encyclopædia Britannica*, Encyclopædia Britannica, Inc., 19 Sept. 2016, www.britannica.com/science/ear-bone.

"Easton's Bible Dictionary Online." Bible Study Tools, www.biblestudytools.com/dictionaries/eastons-bible-dictionary/.

Farbiarz, Rachel. "How Aaron Helped Moses Overcome His Feelings of Inadequacy." *My Jewish Learning*, www.myjewishlearning.com/article/lost-in-translation/.

Goff, Bob. *Everybody Always: Becoming Love in a World Full of Setbacks and Difficult People*. Nelson Books, an Imprint of Thomas Nelson, 2018.

"Graves into Gardens." Lyrics by Chris Brown et al. *Graves into Gardens*, Elevation Worship, 2020.

Henry, Matthew. "Matthew Henry Complete Bible Commentary Online." Bible Study Tools, www.biblestudytools.com/commentaries/matthew-henry-complete/.

Hoffman, Matthew. "Shoulder Human Anatomy: Image, Function, Parts, and More." *WebMD*, WebMD, 18 May 2019, www.webmd.com/pain-management/picture-of-the-shoulder#1.

Hogenboom, Melissa. "Earth - Chins Are a Bit Useless so Why Do We Have Them?" BBC, BBC, 4 Feb. 2016, www.bbc.com/earth/story/20160204-why-do-humans-have-chins.

Mackie, Tim, and Jon Collins. "In the Book of Zephaniah, God's Justice and Love Offer Future Hope.: BibleProject™." *BibleProject*, bibleproject.com/explore/zephaniah/.

Massengale, Tim. *Let My People Grow: a Story of Church Growth*. Word Aflame Press, 1989.

Newman, Tim. "Bones: Types, Structure, and Function." *Medical News Today*, MediLexicon International, 11 Jan. 2018, www.medicalnewstoday.com/articles/320444.

Parilis, Dan. "Singer's Blog." Vocal Brilliance, 9 Nov. 2014, www.vocalbrilliance.com/blog-2/about-blog/.

Cole-Rous, Jim. "Benaiah Son of Jehoiada." *JourneyOnline*, journeyonline.org/lessons/benaiah-son-of-jehoiada/?series=8751.

TerKeurst, Lysa. *Finding I Am: How Jesus Fully Satisfies the Cry of Your Heart*. Lifeway Press, 2017. Print.

A Note from the Author

Dear Reader,

I want to thank you sincerely for supporting my ministry through the purchase of this book. You can follow my Facebook page @MelissaFieldsMinistry and send requests for speaking engagements, singing appointments, and prayer to my inbox there. I am also an author on Goodreads, and I invite you to follow my author profile on that platform as well. If you enjoyed these sermons but have not purchased my first book, The Trouble with Sticks: And Other Lessons from the Bible, I invite you to check it out. It contains 10 sermons as well, and ministers are welcome to use any of them upon purchasing the book. I have included Chapter 1 for you on the remaining pages.

As we emerge from the current pandemic and frenzy that accompanies any election year, I wish health, happiness, and spiritual renewal for you and your family. May God richly bless you!

Sincerely,

Melissa Fields

Chapter One

What Mean These Stones?

And they overcame him by the blood of the Lamb and by the word of their testimony, and they did not love their lives to the death -Revelation 12:11 (NKJV)

It is Memorial Day, 2019, and I am so thankful for men and women who fought for me to have the freedom to write this book. After all, in some countries women are not allowed to be educated, are not allowed to have a voice, are not allowed to be unveiled. Despite how often I stand in my classroom and teach about the barbarism of injustice, I'm always surprised by these truths. One year my students and I read the courageous story of Malala Yousafzai who was shot on a school bus full of young girls by extremists who thought that women did not deserve the liberty that literacy brings. Can you imagine? Being shot simply because you are female and have the audacity to attend school! Sadly, there is a whole world that does not understand Galatians 3:28. Even though I know firsthand the scathing reality of discrimination, I live in a great country where men and women of valor defended my right to liberty and literacy. I have not been denied an education nor have I been denied the freedom of religion that made me a minister in the first place. I have so much to be thankful for.

In Manville, Virginia, yesterday, my father taught a lesson about Memorial Day. He illuminated several Biblical instances where God decreed memorials, remembrances, and tokens. As I listened to his enlightening sermon, these words resonated with me when we passed through the Book of Joshua: "What mean these stones?" As so often happens, the sermon that follows is the result of iron sharpening iron-one minister inspiring another; one Christian sparking another; an Elder rejuvenating an aspiring teacher.

In Joshua 3, the Lord gives the new leader instructions regarding how he and the priests should lead the people into the Promised Land. At the close of that chapter, everything is going as planned. Finally, at the beginning of chapter 4, we read of their success:

1 *And it came to pass, when all the people were clean passed over Jordan, that the Lord spake unto Joshua, saying,* ***2*** *Take you twelve men out of the people, out of every tribe a man,* ***3*** *And command ye them, saying, Take you hence out of the midst of Jordan, out of the place where the priests' feet stood firm, twelve stones, and ye shall carry them over with you, and leave them in the lodging place, where ye shall lodge this night.* ***4*** *Then Joshua called the twelve men, whom he had prepared of the children of Israel, out of every tribe a man:* ***5*** *And Joshua said unto them, Pass over before the ark of the Lord your God into the midst of Jordan, and take you up every man of you a stone upon his shoulder, according unto the number of the tribes of the children of Israel:* ***6*** *That this may be a sign among you, that when your children ask their fathers in time to come,* *saying, What mean ye by these stones?* **7** *Then ye shall answer them, That the waters of Jordan were cut off before the ark of the covenant of the Lord; when it passed over Jordan, the waters of Jordan were cut off: and these stones shall be for a memorial unto the children of Israel for ever.* (KJV)

When my father spoke on Memorial Day, he piqued my interest when he mentioned this story in Joshua. Of course, I had heard it many times, but verse 6 just stayed with me, and I knew the Lord would eventually lead me to study this passage of scripture a little more in depth. I'd like for us to examine the significance of stones in the Bible, and as you might expect, I've entitled this sermon "What Mean These Stones?"

First of all, I would like to point out the beautifully symbolic meaning of this passage. The Jordan marks the place where the Israelites finally left behind their bondage in Egypt and their wandering in the wilderness, crossing over to their freedom in the Promised Land. Of course it was worth erecting a stone memorial to remember this glorious occasion and to honor God for having delivered them. I also find it deeply symbolic that the Lord instructs the men to take stones from the very spot where the priests' feet "stood firm" in the middle of the Jordan. Note that they were told to take these stones upon their shoulders; these weren't tiny pebbles!

I'd like for us to consider some literal attributes of the Jordan River in order for us to understand the significance of these stones. First of all, the Jordan is shallow, but it has a high-water period. The Bible records in chapter 3 that during the time of Joshua's crossing, the river was actually overflowing her banks. The water was brackish and high. Furthermore, "its current is swift and carries a heavy load of silt" ("Jordan River"). If you don't know what silt is, let me throw some synonyms at you: mud, slime, ooze, sludge. The Jordan is even said to be "unnavigable due to its precipitous upper course, its seasonal flow, and its twisting lower course" ("Jordan River").

But God says, "Step into that silty water, into that sludge, trust Me to stop the current, and pull a heavy stone out of the muck. Then place your testimony on dry ground, letting everyone know that I am your God!"

Friends, if we will cling to the place where our High Priest has stood, when we find ourselves in the middle of a mess, we can start looking for those stones. I know that life sometimes seems unnavigable. I know we all, like the Jordan, have times of high-water when we feel we are going to go under. Yet the Bible says that we are overcomers through the word of our testimony. If you concentrate in the midst of your trials, if you can see past the mud and the muck, you will find that you are able to pull your testimony up out of whatever twisting, seemingly unnavigable situation you have found yourself in. He might stop the current or He might simply give you the strength to work against it. The important thing is to look for the Priest's footprints. Which way would Jesus go? I know it is a cliché, but what would He do? How did the priests cross? They were holding the ark of the covenant, and as soon as their feet touched the brim of the waters, God intervened. Stay in covenant with Him, especially when you are facing brackish waters, and pull something great out of your experience with turbulence. It might be heavy; you might have to put your shoulder into it, but Joshua placed 12 stones on an ancient riverbank that say you can! When you are confused, make sure you are in covenant. When you are lost, look for the Priest's footprints!

I find it no surprise that the site of these ancient memorial stones eventually became the historic site of a major moment in another Priest's life, the greatest Priest that ever walked the Earth: Jesus Christ! John the Baptist, in fact, proclaimed Jesus to be the Lamb of God at the Jordan, and he also baptized our Lord in these same waters. In just a little under four years later, another stone would be a marker of the most extraordinary testimony of all time, where once again a Priest was placed.

Consider the first verse of John 20: *The first day of the week cometh Mary Magdalene early, when it was yet dark, unto the sepulchre, and seeth the stone taken away from the sepulchre* (KJV). Talk about someone who needed to see a stone removed! Mary Magdalene had been delivered from demon possession, a veritable spiritual sludge. She knew something about darkness and chaos, but she also knew about covenant. She had been freed from a literal hell and had clung to Jesus, supporting His ministry, since her deliverance. There she was, looking for her High Priest, but the first thing she saw was the stone-the very stone that the Holy Spirit reached down into the darkness of death and hoisted out of those waves of silence. It stands as a testimony that the same Spirit that raised Jesus from the dead can wake us all!

Something miraculous happens when we realize that we are connected through Christ to Resurrection power. Not only does He become our High Priest standing on the stones in the middle of our Jordan, but He actually becomes the Stone Himself. He reigns over everything our feet stand on and everything our shoulders balance. How do I know this? When Peter and John preached the resurrection of the dead in Acts 4, many religious leaders were offended. They had never fathomed that we could die and yet live again. They wanted to silence Peter and John, but that was hard to do given the fact that they kept performing miracles in His name. Let's take a look at the first 11 verses of that chapter (Acts 4):

1 *And as they spake unto the people, the priests, and the captain of the temple, and the Sadducees, came upon them,* ***2*** *Being grieved that they taught the people, and preached through Jesus the resurrection from the dead.* ***3*** *And they laid hands on them, and put them in hold unto the next day: for it was now eventide.* ***4*** *Howbeit many of them which heard the word believed; and the number of the men was about five thousand.* ***5*** *And it came to pass on the morrow, that their rulers, and elders, and scribes,* ***6*** *And Annas the high priest, and Caiaphas, and John, and Alexander, and as many as were of the kindred of the high priest, were gathered together at Jerusalem.* ***7*** *And when they had set them in the midst, they asked, By what power, or by what name, have ye done this?* ***8*** *Then Peter, filled* *with the Holy Ghost, said unto them, Ye rulers of the people, and elders of Israel,* ***9*** *If we this day be examined of the good deed done to the impotent man, by what means he is made whole;****10*** *Be it known unto you all, and to all the people of Israel, that by the name of Jesus Christ of Nazareth, whom ye crucified, whom God raised from the dead, even by him doth this man stand here before you whole.* ***11*** *This is the stone which was set at nought of you builders, which is become the head of the corner.* (KJV)

The New Living Translation of verse 11 might sound a bit more familiar: *For Jesus is the one referred to in the Scriptures, where it says, "The stone that you builders rejected has now become the cornerstone."* The significance of stones in the Bible cannot be denied. Stones marked the spot of victory for Joshua and his people, the resurrection of our Lord, and Christ's place as the principal foundation of truth and power. But there's more. Would you like to hear some really good news today?

I want to stop here and tell you about a powerful spiritual experience that I recently enjoyed. I traveled to Athens and then to the Greek Islands with my colleague and great friend, Rebekah Haren, and 12 students. One of the islands that we visited was the Isle of Patmos where John was exiled for teaching about Jesus. I can't explain how it felt to walk where I know John actually walked, where he actually lived for a time. I am forever grateful that the Saint recorded in Revelation 1:9 his location at the time of the Revelation. While we were on the island, we traveled to the cave where it is believed John received the Apocalypse from

God and actually wrote the visions that later became the last book of our New Testament. There is now a church built around those stone walls, but the cave itself must look much like it did to John centuries ago. So authentic was it that I could not help but weep. Several of our students wept as well. We sat with tears in our eyes and listened to the tour guide speak about John and the words he wrote. The plagues are terrifying. The warnings to the churches are clear. But John also shared some very good news, and guess what? It involves stones. Revelation 2:17 declares: *He that hath an ear, let him hear what the Spirit saith unto the churches; To him that overcometh will I give to eat of the hidden manna, and will give him a white stone, and in the stone a new name written, which no man knoweth saving he that receiveth it* (KJV). Jesus is our High Priest and Chief Cornerstone. In this scripture, He is promising to give us our own stone with a new name if we will overcome the sins of this world and stay true to Him. In ancient times, judges would use white and black pebbles to cast their vote on the innocence or guilt of a person standing trial. If the judge gave the accused a white pebble, it meant the judge was recommending absolution. If, however, the judge gave the accused a black pebble, it meant that the judge believed the accused was guilty. Jesus is telling us if we cling to Him, we will be found innocent simply because He will take our sinful selves and give us a whole new identity. We will eat hidden manna and be given a new name that only we will understand. There are some things, Friends, that are between you and your Savior. There are parts of you that no one knows except Him. Never let anyone discount your walk with God based on what they think they know about you. If you will overcome, if you will trust Him in the mud and muck of your Jordan, when you cross over, He will take your testimony and give you a new name on a white stone. What means that stone? It means victory in Jesus as you sit down to eat Heaven's manna! Reach into the waters and pull out your testimony so that you can trade it one day for an engraved stone!

Dear Reader, I want you to know how much your High Priest loves you. Consider Joshua 4:10. "For the priests which bare the ark stood in the midst of Jordan, until every thing was finished that the Lord commanded..." The priests stood firm until it was finished. Isn't that just like our Jesus? Never relenting on the cross, crying out to our souls that "It is finished!"

Made in the USA
Columbia, SC
28 October 2020

23615390R00083